Just Dirt on the Dress

GINA NEW SHUMPERT

ISBN 978-1-64079-388-0 (paperback)
ISBN 978-1-64079-389-7 (digital)

Copyright © 2017 by Gina New Shumpert

All rights reserved. No part of this publication may be reproduced, distributed, or transmitted in any form or by any means, including photocopying, recording, or other electronic or mechanical methods without the prior written permission of the publisher. For permission requests, solicit the publisher via the address below.

Christian Faith Publishing, Inc.
832 Park Avenue
Meadville, PA 16335
www.christianfaithpublishing.com

Printed in the United States of America

ACKNOWLEDGMENTS

First and foremost, I am thankful that God spoke this Bible study into my heart and revealed to me the words to say. The romance I felt throughout this journey was truly remarkable! Each word typed was exhilarating. When I spoke the words in Isaiah 6:8, "Here Am I. Send me," God answered and allowed me to be a vessel in spreading the good news and hope to others. Thank you, Lord, for loving me, saving me, and allowing me to be used by You for Your Glory!

Thanks to my wonderful husband, Jera, who is my answered prayer when I prayed that God would send someone who would love me as I sat at home alone on junior prom night. You are the husband in Ephesians 5:25! An ocean full of thanks goes to the one who is my encourager, supporter, empty-nest companion, my mood lifter, shoulder to cry on, my earthly example of unconditional love each day, and my joy. Your never-ending support of anything that I do is greatly appreciated. Your laughter is contagious. Thanks for always making me laugh but never laughing at me. Your love keeps me on cloud nine!

Thanks to Jana and Jake who truly showed me what God's unconditional love was all about! You both fill my heart with tremendous love! I'm forever grateful that God allowed me to be your mom. What joy you give me each and every day! I love you to the moon and back a thousand times!

To all of my family and friends, I want to thank you. Each of you has played a special part in my life's journey. Sharing yourself with me has helped me become who I am today. I take a piece of you with me wherever I go. Love you all dearly!

CONTENTS

Preface 5

Week 1		Just	
	Day 1	Just as I Am 9
	Day 2	Just with God 16
	Day 3	Just as If 23
	Day 4	Justice 33
	Day 5	Justify 41

Week 2		Dirt	
	Day 1	Dig in the Dirt 49
	Day 2	Iniquity to Influence 58
	Day 3	Renew 66
	Day 4	Tree of Life 75
	Day 5	Yoke to Yearn 85

Week 3		On	
	Day 1	On Guard 93
	Day 2	On Christ the Solid Rock I Stand 100
	Day 3	On the Lookout 107
	Day 4	On Cloud Nine 113
	Day 5	Onward Christian Soldier 118

Week 4		The	
	Day 1	The Jesus Is Thy Lord 129
	Day 2	The One and Only 136
	Day 3	The Indescribable Gift 143

Day 4	The Lord Is My Shepherd	150
Day 5	The Other Side	154
Week 5	**Dress**	
Day 1	Dressed in His Glory	163
Day 2	Radiant	169
Day 3	Exquisite	177
Day 4	Song of Solomon	182
Day 5	Saved, Sanctified, and Set Free	191
References		201

PREFACE

It was the first wedding gown I tried on the day I went wedding dress shopping. It fit perfectly. I just had to have it! It made me feel like a princess. Later, I would realize why it was such a great price. There were two small dirty spots on my otherwise gorgeous white wedding gown. Those two blots stuck out at me like a sore thumb. Even my matron of honor noticed them on my wedding day regardless of the fact that I had the dress cleaned. I rationalized those two blemishes in the gown as symbolic of my own blemishes and shortcomings. I wanted to feel pure and as white as newly fallen snow on my wedding day. My soon-to-be husband and I had waited so long for this special day. From the very first time of reading *Cinderella*, I had dreamt of my own Prince Charming carrying me off to our palace and living happily ever after.

"Just dirt on the dress" is a phrase that my dear friend said to me when I shared my life story with her. Just like any life story, it is filled with good and bad times, happy moments, and life-changing trials. Unfortunately, I carried those blots around with me like an old, ragged coat that I couldn't bear to part with. As a German shepherd sheds his winter coat each year, it was time for me to shed that coat for good. I had walked around wounded from life's trials for far too long. This is a journey from being a broken girl—never feeling quite good enough to becoming a radiant bride of Christ, made perfect by the blood of Jesus. God's awesome power can change anyone from a life of sin, self-condemnation, and brokenness to living an abundant life for Him and for His Glory. I'm audaciously living out His story for me.

This is a Bible study that takes you on a journey of redemption. Everyone must come to the realization of the need to come to Jesus just as he is. We do not have to have all of the answers or get everything in order before coming to Jesus. The next step is to realize what the dirt or sin in our life consists of in order to rid it from our lives. When we do that, we can draw closer to God. Finally, we are the Bride of Christ, dressed in a Robe of Righteousness, awaiting the great day of our Lord Jesus Christ's return when we are set free for all eternity.

Each chapter in my story displays God's immeasurable grace. God promises to "work all things together for good to those who love the Lord and are called according to His purpose" (Rom. 8:28). I anxiously await the next chapter God unveils to me as he promised in the Bible: "For I know the plans I have for you, declares the Lord, plans to prosper you and not to harm you, plans to give you hope and a future" (Jer. 29:11).

WEEK 1

Just

DAY 1

Just as I Am

If we confess our sins, He is faithful and righteous to forgive us our sins and to cleanse us from all unrighteousness.
—1 John 1:9

Why Did God Provide a Way of Salvation for Each of Us?

Welcome to *Just Dirt on the Dress* Bible study. I'm delighted that you have decided to take this journey with me. This is a study encompassing the life of a Christian—from accepting Jesus just as you are, to walking faithfully and being on the lookout for God's blessings, to finally reaching our eternal home as the Bride of Christ.

There are many themes throughout this study, but the overarching theme is that we are the beautiful Bride of Christ. We are not worthy on our own to be His Bride. It is only through the forgiveness of our sins by the blood of Christ that we become worthy, blameless, and without blemish. Through the saving grace of Jesus, God sees us as radiant and exquisite. Now, get your Bibles handy—and perhaps even a dictionary—and let us begin this awesome journey of growth in faith, hope, and love.

I remember my baptism as if it were yesterday even though it has been over thirty years since I began my walk with Jesus. "Now I belong to Jesus! Jesus belongs to me. Not for the years of time alone but for eternity," the congregation sang as I came out of the water of baptism. The words floated through the air like balloons and touched my soul. As I was raised out of the baptismal, the faint chant of "Gina! Gina! Gina!" resonated throughout the room from a precocious two-year-old. "Jesus belongs to me," echoed in the room alongside the faint call of my name over and over.

The feeling of being released from the chains of guilt and shame washed over me. That Christmas Eve was different. I had received the best present ever, the indescribable gift of everlasting life! Jesus made it possible. He washed all the dirty sins away—the sins of yesterday, today and tomorrow. My sins were just dirt on the dress washed out by the blood of Jesus.

Just as God sacrificed an animal and shed its blood to cover Adam and Eve after the first sin, God sacrificed His one and only son to cover our sins. We were made clean by the blood of Jesus and continually remain as white as snow, pure and blameless. Just as I am, I came to Jesus, and He accepted me that way.

Read Acts 22:16, Matthew 3:2 and John 3:5. What insights do you gain from these verses?

_____
_____
_____

The ever-important question that's asked when someone comes forward to give their life to Christ is, *Do you believe that Jesus is the Christ, the Son of the Living God?* Yes! Yes! Yes!

Do you believe, my friend? Have you been baptized into Christ? Do you have the blessed assurance that you belong to Jesus and will spend eternity with Him in Heaven?

Do not delay in accepting Jesus as your Lord and Savior—repent and be baptized today! Oh, how we long for all sinners to be converted. How our hearts ache for you who are still lost, particularly those closest to us! You do not have to get everything right in your life before accepting His free gift of salvation, and there is nothing in your past too dirty or stained that cannot be removed by Jesus. The Christian walk is a journey. You take one step of faith at a time.

Perhaps you've been a Christian for years like me. Then, you too continually come to Jesus just as you are. As we learn in the Bible, "For all have sinned and fallen short of the glory of God" (Rom. 3:23). God's grace "will cover a multitude of sins" (James 5:20). Tell Him everything, confess your sins daily, and don't beat yourself up for not being perfect. Only Jesus lived as a perfect man. There is no other like Him. All of us must realize the importance of our need for repentance: "If we confess our sins, He is faithful and righteous to forgive us our sins and to cleanse us from all unrighteousness" (1 John 1:9).

What does it mean to "confess our sins?"

_____
_____
_____

If you were to explain 1 John 1:9 to someone who didn't understand it, what would you say?

_____
_____
_____

According to *Merriam-Webster*, *to confess* is a transitive verb meaning "to admit that you did something wrong or illegal"; "to talk about or admit something that makes you embarrassed, ashamed, etc.; and to tell (your sins) to God."

Children love to tell on each other when they catch someone doing something inappropriate. As children of God, we should not look for the errors of others. We need to examine ourselves. It's as simple as just telling on yourself to God. He already knows, but He wants to hear it from us. Total and complete forgiveness is within our reach. You just need the right equation:

Confession + His Righteousness = Total Forgiveness

Recall your baptism and describe it in the margin. If you have not been baptized, what is holding you back?

_____
_____
_____

What insights do you gain from the following scriptures about confession?

- Psalm 32:5

- Matthew 3:6

- Matthew 10:32

- Romans 10:9

- James 5:16

- 2 Corinthians 9:13

Think about your sins that need to be confessed. Write them down if you wish. Then get on your knees and ask God to forgive you of those sins.

_____
_____
_____

Read Psalm 51:1-13 prayerfully.

This passage of scripture, according to *hannahscupboard.com*, was a plea from King David to the Lord for forgiveness. He had sinned with Bathsheba and had been called to account for it by Nathan the prophet. David is asking for deep heart cleansing and uses hyssop to symbolize that since it is a common cleaning agent. It is interesting that when he says "wash me" he is talking about the way clothes were washed in his time, with beating and pounding. He is so deeply sorry, he wants more than a quick wash up. He wants the very desire for sin to be washed out of him.

Have you ever felt that repentant over your own sin?

_____
_____
_____

When I continually commit the same cycle of sins, I get to the point where I just beg to have those things beat out of me. I'm tired of falling into the same pit of sin time and time again. Wash it out of me, Lord!

Notice all of the words referring to being cleansed that are used in Psalm 51:1–13. What are they?

_____
_____
_____

Uses of *blot (out)* as a verb in the Old Testament are all translated from the Hebrew word *machah*. The website Jesus-resurrection.info defines it as "to wipe, to wipe out"; "to be blotted out, to be exterminated."

The phrase *purify with hyssop* caught my attention. According the hannahscupboard.com, *hyssop* is a common herb which grew in Bible times and still grows extensively today in many varieties all over the world. Common varieties grow to about two feet tall and spread about a foot. It has beautiful purple-blue flowers and a strong minty smell. Because it had detergent properties, it was widely used to clean sacred places such as temples.

Here are some examples of when hyssop was used in the Bible:

- A bunch of hyssop was used to dip in the basin of blood of the Passover lamb to apply to the lintel and doorpost before the Israelites left Egypt in Exodus 12:22. Since hyssop has strong, woody stalks, it could stand up to being shaken.
- The cleansing ceremony for a leper in Leviticus 14:1-8. Again, hyssop was the dipping agent into blood of a bird and used to sprinkle over the unclean person.
- In John 19:29, it was used at the crucifixion: "Now a vessel full of sour wine was sitting there, and they filled a sponge with sour wine, put it on hyssop, and put it to His mouth."

It is my desire for God to blot out my transgressions, cleanse me from my sin, purify me with hyssop, and wipe the slate or in this case my heart and soul clean.

What is the definition of clean?

_____

_____

_____

I do not usually buy white clothing simply for the reason that I know I will eventually stain it up with something such as my coffee, tea, or breakfast. According to rodalesorganiclife.com, the number 1 way to have a cleaner load of laundry was to soak stains immediately: "'When you get a stain on something, you have to deal with it immediately,' says Green. If you let it dry, it's permanent. When spills happen, Green recommends leaving the soiled article of clothing in a bucket full of water with a little detergent added until you have time to treat the stain."

If we use this scenario to relate it to our Christian walk, we would say it this way: Go to Jesus for the bucket washing through baptism. Allow Him to soak the stains clean with His detergent known as the blood that was shed for each of us. And then continue to go to Jesus with every stain to let Him deal with it immediately before it has a chance of becoming a permanent stain on your heart. Jesus cleans it just right!

Highlight the words that represent being clean:

pure	upstanding	righteous
virtuous	upright	spotless
contaminated	tainted	dirty
honest	unadulterated	stained

"Create in me a clean heart, O God, and renew a steadfast spirit within me," the Bible says in Psalm 51:10. Oh, how we wish for our hearts to be clean and stay clean. If we just repent daily of our sins, then we can have that same fresh, clean feeling we had right after baptism each and every day.

The word *love* is written 310 times in the Bible in the King James Version—131 times in the Old Testament and 179 times in the New Testament. It increases in the NIV with 319 in the Old Testament and 232 times in the New Testament for a grand total of 551 times christianbiblereference.org. I would agree that God's love abounds more and more.

Circle every form of the word love in the following verses:

- I have loved you with an everlasting love; therefore I have drawn you with lovingkindness. (Jer. 31:3)
- I love those who love me; and those who diligently seek me will find me. (Prov. 8:17)
- Hatred stirs up strife, but love covers all transgressions. (Prov. 10:12)
- For God so loved the world, that He gave His only begotten son, that whoever believes in Him should not perish, but have eternal life. (John 3:16)
- Just as He chose us in Him before the foundation of the world, that we should be holy and without blame before Him in love. (Eph. 1:4)
- Above all, keep fervent in your love for one another, because love covers a multitude of sins. (1 Pet. 4:8)
- The one who does not love does not know God, for God is love. (1 John 4:8)

Do you feel God's love for you? If not, what is keeping you from feeling loved by God?

_____
_____
_____

Why did God provide a way of salvation for us?

_____

_____

_____

I pray that you feel God's love for you more and more with each passing day.

When we confess our sins, they are washed clean, and our relationship with God is restored. Jesus allows us to put on the gorgeous white wedding gown known as the Robe of Righteousness because of what He did for each of us. He makes us whiter than snow. Jesus gives us forgiveness and hope by His willingness to die on the cross as punishment for our sins. He is the one who blots out, cleanses, cleans, and purifies our souls. Jesus renews us and restores us to a right relationship with God. Jesus is the reason we should feel incredibly loved by God because "greater love has no one than this, that one lay down his life for his friends" (John 15:13).

Come just as you are to the best friend you will ever have. God loves you just as you are. Perfection is not a requirement for His love. Come, radiant bride, your Beloved is waiting! Remember this from the Bible: "I will give thanks to the Lord with all my heart; I will tell of all Thy wonders. I will be glad and exult in Thee. I will sing praise to Thy Name, O Most High" (Ps. 9:1-2).

Music touches the depths of our soul much greater than words ever could. As Johann Sebastian Bach once said, "Music is an agreeable harmony for the honor of God and the permissible delights of the soul."

I have chosen a song for each day that has special meaning to me and felt was relevant for the topic of the day. Likewise, you choose a song for each day that touches your heart and soul.

My song of the day: "Something in the Water" by Carrie Underwood
Your song of the day: _____

DAY 2

Just with God

How then can a man be just with God? Or how can he be clean who is born of woman?
—Job 25:4

How Do You Become Just with God?

Do you remember a time when you made a bad choice and your parents found out? Recall that feeling of knowing you disappointed your parents. Yes, they still love you, but the feeling that things just aren't quite right sweeps over you. All you want to do is fix it back to where things were prior to that bad choice.

Just with God refers to wanting things to be right with God. We are sinners, each one. We all fall short of the glory of God and sin separates us from God, and our "iniquities have made a separation between you and your God, and your sins have hidden His face from you, so that He does not hear" (Isa. 59:2).

Sin separates us from God. How can we fix it? How can we make it right? We can't, but Jesus can! Sin separates us from God, but nothing separates us from His love! We are told in Romans 8:38-39,

> For I am convinced that neither death, nor life, nor angels, nor principalities, nor things present, nor things to come, nor powers, nor height, nor depth, nor any other created thing, shall be able to separate us from the love of God, which is in Christ Jesus our Lord.

Just run to Jesus and He will fix it.

Read Psalm 103:12. How far have our transgressions been removed from us?

JUST DIRT ON THE DRESS

Read 1 Peter 3:18. Fill in the missing words: "For Christ also died for sins once for all, the _____ for the _____, in order that He might bring us to God, having been put to death in the flesh, but made alive in the spirit."

Who is the one just is referring to in this scripture? _____

Who are the unjust referred to in this scripture? _____

Write the definition of *just*.

_____
_____
_____

According to *Dictionary.com, just* means "guided by truth, reason, justice, and fairness"; "it's done or made according to principle; equitable; proper." The Google definition of *just* is "based on or behaving according to what is morally right and fair." Jesus was always guided by truth, especially during His forty days of temptation. He fought Satan back with the word of God, never faltering. He never sinned.

The prefix *un* means "not"; therefore, the unjust are not just, right, fair, or proper. Christ, being just, died for all of us who are the unjust in order to make us alive in the spirit and just with God (1 Pet. 3:18.)

Read Ecclesiastes 12:14 and Psalm 51:6. What is the common denominator in these two scriptures?

_____
_____
_____

God knows it all—the good, the bad, the ugly, and the really ugly. He knows everything, including the things we try to hide. Christ died in order to make us right with God. Nothing is hidden from God. He knows it all as said in Matthew 5:45, "He makes His sun rise on the evil and on the good, and sends rain on the just and on the unjust." John MacArthur puts it this way: "But His love provided a remedy for sin through the atoning works of Jesus Christ on behalf of all who repent of their sins and trust in His way. Therefore, John 3:16!"

Reread 1 Peter 3:18 and fill in the missing words: "For Christ also died for sins once for all, the just for the unjust, in order that He might _____ ___ ___ _____, having been put to death in the flesh, but made alive in the spirit."

Jesus brought us back to a right relationship with God: "Truly, truly, I say to you, he who hears My word, and believes Him who sent Me, has eternal life, and does not come into judgment, but has passed out of death into life" (John 5:24).

How do you become just with God?

_____
_____
_____

How can he be clean who is born of woman?

_____
_____
_____

> For I know my transgressions, and my sin is ever before me. Against Thee, Thee only, I have sinned, and done what is evil in thy sight, so that Thou art justified when Thou dost speak. And blameless when Thou dost judge (Ps. 51:3-4).

David's sin was ever before him; likewise, we need to reflect and make our sins ever before us. We need to acknowledge our transgressions. As stated on biblehub.com,

> The first step in repentance is contrition; the second, confession; the third, amendment of life. I bear it in mind; I do not hide it from myself. I keep it continually before my mental vision. This, too, is characteristic of true penitence. Mock penitents confess their sins, and straightway forget them. Real genuine ones find it impossible to forget.

Compare the following scriptures. What insights do you gain?

Romans 2:28-29

Galatians 3:26-29

Ephesians 1:7

Ephesians 1:13-14

Through faith in our Lord Jesus Christ, we are all children of God and are clothed in His Robe of Righteousness, forgiven of our sins, sealed with the Holy Spirit, and with the promise of a great inheritance awaiting us.

Read Psalm 103:11-22. How great is His lovingkindness towards those who fear Him?

_____
_____
_____

What does the Lord, our Father, have for those who fear Him?

_____
_____
_____

God loves us and has compassion for those who fear Him and keep His word. Fear in this context is to revere as said in the Bible: "Worship the Lord with reverence, and rejoice with trembling" (Ps. 2:11). Muster all of the respect and reverence you can gather for the Almighty, all-powerful, wonderful, awesome God that He is. Be like the woman in Proverbs 31:30: "Charm is deceitful and beauty is vain, but a woman who fears the Lord, she shall be praised." My dear sister in Christ, revere the one and only true God!

Read Jeremiah 7:23 and Revelation 22:7; 12-17. Check all that apply according to Psalm 103:11-22, Jeremiah 7:23, Revelation 22:7, and Revelation 22:12-17:

Our Heavenly Father	Christians
___Compassionate	___Obey Voice of God
___Loving	___Stay Silent
___Everlasting	___Heeds God's Word
___Trustworthy	___Bless the Lord
___Keeps promises (covenants)	___Fear God
___Mighty in Strength	___Blessed
___Alpha and Omega	___God's people

According to Jeremiah 7:23, what did God say to do in order that "it may be well with you?"

_____
_____
_____

Fill in the blanks of what we gain by being In Christ:

"But by His doing you are in Christ Jesus, who became to us _____ from God, and _____ and _____, and _____. 1 Corinthians 1:30

What does the phrase "who became to us wisdom from God" mean to you?
_____
_____
_____

Define the following words:
Righteousness:_____
_____
_____

Sanctification:_____
_____
_____

Redemption:_____
_____
_____

When we are in Christ, we are redeemed and made righteous; totally and completely free from guilt or sin. The dirt on the dress of our soul is as white as snow. Our virtuous lives continue to grow in divine grace. Through this sanctification, we draw closer each day to being more like Jesus. Make it your goal to love Jesus more with each passing day.

According to Revelation 22:14, who has the right to the tree of life and the ability to enter by the gates into the city?
_____
_____
_____

How do we get our robes washed?
_____
_____
_____

Fill in the missing words for the following scriptures:

- And behold, I am _____ quickly. Blessed is he who heeds the words of the prophecy of this book. (Rev. 22:7)
- And the Spirit and the bride say, _____. And let the one who hears say, _____. And let the one who is thirsty _____; let the one who wishes take the water of life without cost. (Rev. 22:17)
- He who testifies to these things says, 'Yes! I am _____ quickly.' Amen. _____, Lord Jesus. (Rev. 22:20)

There is no "save the date" for our wedding as the Bride of Christ. One of Satan's greatest tricks of deception is to convince you that you have all the time in the world to get things right with God. Do not wait any longer before accepting Jesus. As said in scripture, "Behold, I am coming quickly. Blessed is he who heeds the words of the prophecy of this book" (Rev. 22:7). He's coming—quickly! Be ready!

Allow Jesus to do some cleaning on your soul so that you may be just with God. Walk in the way which God commanded you (Jer. 7:23), and then you will be satisfied, whole, and blameless with a new heart and spirit. Bride of Christ, be joyful in God just like Hannah displays in this passage of scripture: "Then Hannah prayed and said, 'My heart exults in the Lord; my horn is exalted in the Lord; my mouth speaks boldly against my enemies, because I rejoice in Thy salvation" (1 Sam. 2:1).

The only way man or woman can be just with God is simply by accepting the free gift of salvation offered by Jesus as said in Proverbs 4:18: "The path of the just is as the shining light, that shineth more and more unto the perfect day." Keep shining, radiant bride, for Jesus! "Let us come before Him with thanksgiving and extol Him with music and song" (Ps. 95:2).

My song of the day: "East to West" by Casting Crowns
Your song of the day: _____

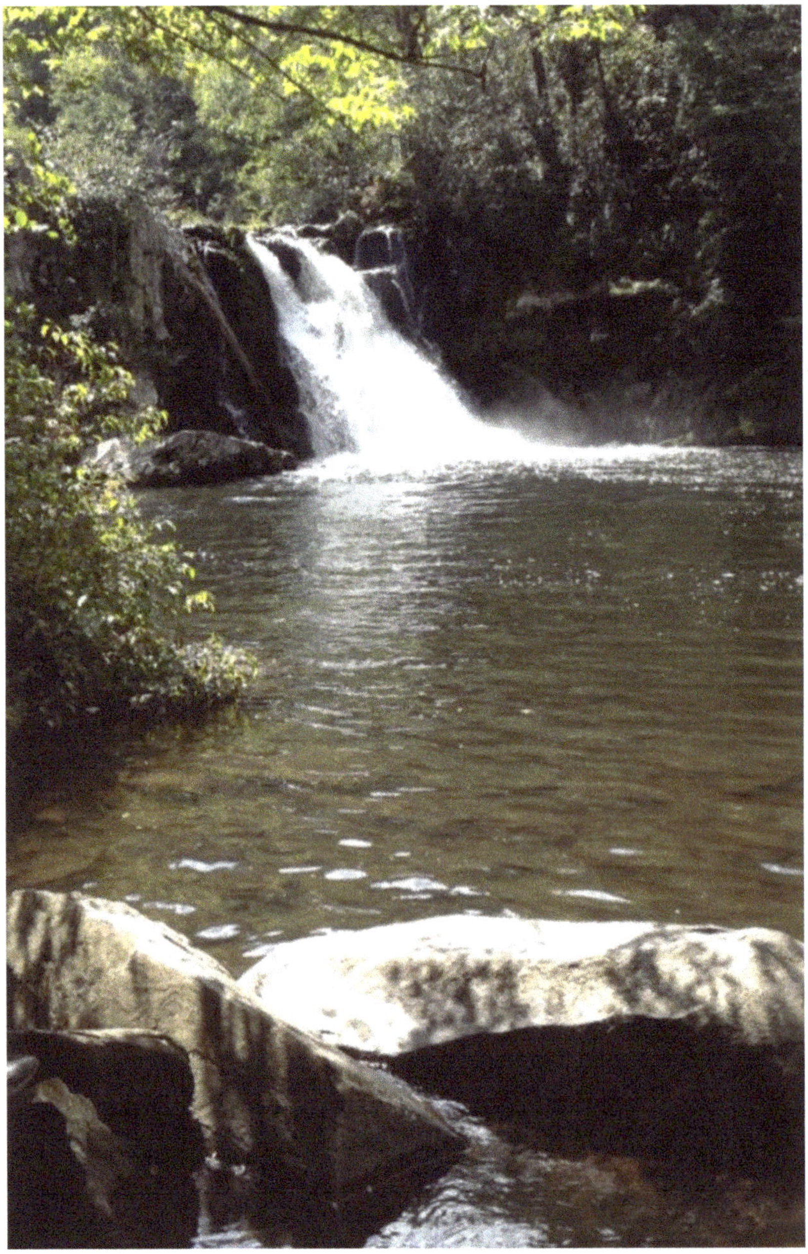

DAY 3

Just as If

*He made Him who knew no sin to be sin on our behalf, that
we might become the righteousness of God in Him.*
—2 Corinthians 5:21

How Would Our Lives Be Different
if Jesus Chose Not to Die for Us?

Do you recall when you first started dating? Were there times when you could not think of anything or anyone else? Would you doodle his name with hearts around it? Is there a tree somewhere with a heart shape carved in it with initials declaring your love for each other? Are there scraps of paper with what you hope will be your future new married name written on them?

There is a spring in your step and joy glowing on your face when you are in love. It is just as if you have forgotten about everything else around you. Your enthusiastic spirit is evident to all. It's just as if your heart will explode with joy! Your smile can be seen for miles. May you never lose that, radiant bride.

Jesus treats me just as if I have never sinned. His heart for each of us never changes. We, too, need to have a heart like Jesus. I was tainted, but He treats me just as if it never happened. What evil meant for harm, God turned it around to be used for good. Jesus treats me as if I am perfect; however, He is the only one who is perfect. Yet Jesus was the one treated just as if He was the sinner, the liar, and the cheater. His sacrifice on the cross gives us a new heart and spirit of righteousness. No longer are we unworthy, broken, blemished, blotted, or stained. Jesus makes Christians just as if we had never been anything but pure and innocent like the day we were born.

According to wordreference.com, the definition of *as if* is "as though;" "in such a way that"; "like, or just like." Some synonyms found on thesaurus.com are "as it were, as it would be"; "in such a way that"; and "just as though."

Does your behavior toward others waver based on your feelings? How many times have misunderstandings occurred simply because of jealousy or insecurity? How many times have you not treated someone the way you usually would if it had not been for those feelings? Does it waver when they have hurt you, not called you, or disappoint you in some way?

Combat those feelings of jealousy, strife, and dissension. What if we treated others just as if they never annoyed, irritated, or hurt us? We are to do to others as you would have them do to you (Luke 6:31). We can combat those feelings of dissension by getting our heart right, by being filled with the Holy Spirit, and by remembering that all of us make mistakes but were made blameless. Let's love others the way that Jesus loves each of us. Jesus's love for us never wavers. It is just as if you get the biggest smile from Him every time you meet Him.

What if we treated everyone just as if they are our one and only, our joy, and our BFF? What would that look like?

_____
_____
_____

Read Romans 10:8-15. What does it say?

_____
_____
_____

First, you must believe in your heart that Jesus is Lord who died and rose from the dead to offer salvation to everyone. Next, you must be willing to confess that truth to others. When we believe in Jesus, we will not be disappointed (Rom. 10:11). Allow your heart to believe in the almighty saving power of Jesus! Then, confess it with your mouth and share the "glad tiding of good things" to everyone you meet (Rom. 10:15, NASB).

Create your own visuals from Romans 10:8-15 like the following to make succinct points given about the heart.

Heart = seed of belief
Heart = conscience

Keeping the law is not equal to justification with God, but having faith in Jesus and His sacrifice for us will provide that justification, our salvation. Have a heart for Jesus. Love Him with all of your heart. Always keep your heart open to Jesus. He loves you, died for you, and treats you just as if you have never sinned.

The word *heart* is mentioned 830 times in KJV, and it can be used as a noun or a verb (christianbiblereference.org). The heart is a hollow organ that pumps the blood through the circulatory system by rhythmic contraction and dilation. In vertebrates, there may be up to four chambers (as in humans), with two atria and two ventricles. The heart can also mean the central or innermost part of something such as the heart of the city (Merriam-Webster Dictionary). A heart symbol is also used to show that you like or love something or someone very much. I use the heart symbol every day when I text my loved ones.

The first mention of *heart* in the Bible is in Genesis 6:5. The second is like it in Genesis 8:21. What similarities do you find in these two verses?

_____
_____
_____

Due to free will, each of us has the tendency to sin and have a heart that can lead us astray. Keep in mind, "Your heart is an organ, keep it in tune with Jesus" (Verlyn D. Verbrugge).

Read Joel 2:12-13. Joel calls on the people of Judah to repent and turn to the Lord. Here too is another example of keeping your heart in check. What are we to do with our hearts according to James 5:8?

_____
_____
_____

To help strengthen our hearts, what are we *not* to do according to James 5:9?

_____
_____
_____

Read 2 Corinthians 5:21 and 2 Corinthians 7:1. How do these verses resonate with you?

_____
_____
_____

It's imperative that we hide scriptures in our heart to resist temptations. Read the following scriptures and write one word that describes the heart in each passage:

- Psalm 51:10 _____
- Psalm 57:7 _____
- Psalm 73:1 _____
- Proverbs 17:22 _____
- Ecclesiastes 8:5 _____
- Matthew 5:8 _____

Which verse or verses resonate with you the most? Why?
_____
_____
_____

"Ezekiel 36 foretells the end-time repentance, conversion, and transformation of Israel. Of course, the offer from God to 'give you a new heart and put a new spirit within you' (v.26) ultimately applies to all people, since all people will be invited to become a part of Israel in a spiritual sense," as referenced to at bible.ucg.org.

Read Ezekiel 36:25-28. When Israel returned to the Lord, what things were given to them according to Ezekiel 36:25-28?
_____
_____
_____

In Ezekiel 36:26, it states that God will give us a new heart and put a new spirit within us. Because of salvation through the blood of Jesus, we have the promise of getting rid of the stone in our heart and receiving a new heart.
We trade a heart of STONE

    Sins
    Transgressions
    Obstinacies
    Negativity
    Egotism

for a new heart

    New self

Eternal life
Wisdom

Hope
Endearment
Adoration
Reverence
Truth

NEW + HEART - STONE = HEART OF FLESH

Hope
Endearment
Adoration
Reverence
Truth

Overflowing goodness & mercy
Freedom

Favor with God
Love
Eternal Life
Salvation
Heaven as a destination

This acrostic is what I came up with to demonstrate what we give up when you have a heart for Jesus and the many blessings we gain as a result. Create your own acrostic for *heart of flesh* to symbolize what you gain by being a child of God.

Reflect on all of the promises you have when Jesus removes the stone and gives you a heart of flesh. Describe what you are feeling in the margin and/or draw a symbol beside each term in the acrostic.

What have you gained by Jesus dying for you?
_____

Read 1 Peter 2:9-10 and fill in the missing words: "But you are a _____ race, a _____ priesthood, a _____ nation, a people for God's _____ _____, that you may proclaim the excellencies of Him who has _____ you out of _____ into His marvelous _____; for you once were not a people, but now you are the _____ ____ _____; you had not received mercy, but now you _____ _____ _____."

Read Ephesians 3:14-21. What are we promised to receive when we accept salvation?
_____
_____
_____

According to Ephesians 3:14-21, how can we as Christians be strengthened with power?
_____

Be Filled with the Spirit

Read Matthew 1:20. Jesus is of the Holy Spirit.

Be filled with the Holy Spirit not a religious spirit. R. Joyner believes

> a religious spirit keeps us from hearing the voice of God by encouraging us to assume that we already know God's opinion, what He is saying, and what pleases Him. The motivation of the Holy Spirit is love for the son of God.

Read Ephesians 5:18-21. According to Ephesians 5:18-21, what are some examples of the outward expressions of being filled with the spirit?
_____
_____
_____

Are you encouraging one another with psalms, hymns, and spiritual songs? ____

Are you making melody in your heart to the Lord? ____

Do you always give thanks for all things in the name of our Lord Jesus Christ to God? ____

Are you subject to one another? Do you look out for one another? ____

Does it say anywhere in those verses to have a spirit of haughtiness or a judgmental spirit? ____

The Holy Spirit is called "the Helper." Allow the Holy Spirit to help you in your Christian walk. Listen ever so closely.

Read John 14:26, and then fill in the missing words: "But the _____, the _____ _____, whom the Father will send in My name, He will _____ you all things, and _____ to your _____ all that I said to you."

Read Romans 8:26-27. Fill in the missing words: "And in the same way the Spirit also _____ our weakness; for we do not know how to _____ as we should, but the Spirit Himself _____ for us with groanings too deep for words; and He who _____ the hearts knows what the mind of the Spirit is, because He _____ for the saints according to the _____ of _____."

Read Matthew 3:11. What does this verse say about the Holy Spirit?

_____
_____
_____

Read Matthew 10:20. Then, fill in the missing words: "For it is not you who speak, but it is the _____ of your _____ who speaks in you."

Warning: Do not resist the Holy Spirit. Read Acts 7:51.

Remember that God is with us. Allow His Spirit to lead and guide you each day. Remember what Henry David Thoreau says: "What lies behind us and what lies before us are tiny matters compared to what lies within us."

Blameless

Jesus treats us just as if we are blameless. Read Proverbs 11:20 and Psalm 119:80. What similarities do you find in these two verses?

_____
_____
_____

Read the following verses: Job 4:17; 1 Corinthians 1:8; Ephesians 1:4; Philippians 2:15; and Jude 24-25. How are we as Christians described?

_____
_____
_____

What If?

When my children were young, we would play the what-if game. The children would ask me what if questions such as

> What if the sky were purple?
> What if I could fly?
> What if Jesus came back today?

Thankfully, as Christians we do not have to ask the following what-if questions: *What if Jesus did not love me? What if Jesus did not die for my sins? What if I were lost for eternity?*

Complete the following what-if verses:

John 8:31—"If you abide in My word, then _____."

John 15:7—"If you abide in Me, and My words abide in you, _____
_____."

Matthew 6:14-15—"For if you forgive men for their transgressions, _____
_____."

Matthew 21:21-22—"And Jesus answered and said to them, 'Truly, I say to you, if you have faith, and do not doubt, you _____
_____
_____."

John 11:40—"Jesus said to her, 'Did I not say to you, if you believe, _____
_____."

John 13:35—"_____, if you have love for one another."

John 14:15—"If you love Me, _____."

Romans 8:31—"What then shall we say to these things? If God is for us, _____
_____?"

Romans 10:9—"That if you confess with your mouth Jesus as Lord, and believe in your heart that God raised Him from the dead, _____."

JUST DIRT ON THE DRESS

2 Corinthians 5:17—"Therefore if any man is in Christ, _____
_____
_____."

Suppose Jesus chose not to die for us. How would our lives be different?
_____
_____
_____

Now, take a few moments and just ponder Jesus for a little while. Say a prayer of thanks to Jesus for the gift of salvation.

Fill in the blanks of what we gain by being In Christ: "But by His doing you are in Christ Jesus, who became to us _____ from God, and _____ and _____, and _____. (1 Cor. 1:30)

What are we to do according to Ephesians 4:32? _____ _____ and _____ to _____ _____, _____ each other, just as in Christ God forgave you.

Here's one final equation for the day: Faith + Jesus = salvation

Jesus treats each of us with love, compassion, and kindness. He is forgiving and tenderhearted and treats each of us as if we've never made a mistake. He placed the stained clothes upon Himself and keeps us dressed in a brilliantly white Robe of Righteousness (at all times!)

Go ahead. Start doodling your name with *Jesus. Jesus loves me*. Draw hearts all around it declaring that He loves you, that He died for you! Give Jesus your full attention as taught to us in Matthew 22:37: "Love the Lord your God with all your heart and with all your soul and with all your mind." God will restore your soul and make it just as if there were no sin stains on it at all.

As we close the lesson of the day, pray each day to love Jesus and others the way that He would. Treat everyone in such a way that they will say you are the friend that everyone wished they had. "The Lord is my strength and song, and He has become my salvation; this is my God, and I will praise Him; my father's God, and I will extol Him" (Exod. 15:2)

My song of the day: "Redeemed" by Big Daddy Weave
Your song of the day: _____

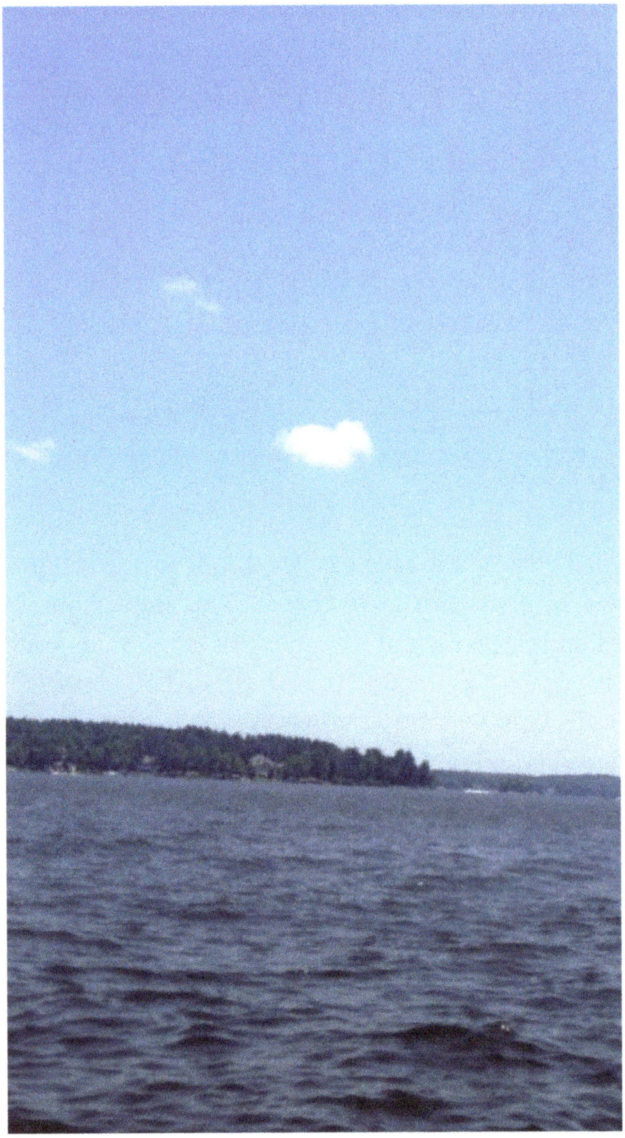

DAY 4

Justice

He has told you, O man, what is good; and what does the Lord require of you but to do justice, to love kindness, and to walk humbly with your God?
—Micah 6:8

Why Does Everyone Expect Life to be Fair?

Have you ever had someone, even a wonderful friend, disappoint you? It hurts when a once-dear friend calls out of the blue after a span of years have gone by without so much as a peep because she needs a favor. I usually help out because I believe that is what Jesus would do; however, it leaves a stinging pain in my heart because I feel used. Perhaps, I have high expectations of people.

Why do I automatically expect them to handle a situation the same way that I would? I expect a reply when I call or text, I expect you to keep your appointment with me, and I expect you to want to talk to me or be with me simply for the joy of spending time with me and not because you need something from me. Am I wrong?

R. Joyner once said, "When we criticize someone, we are in effect declaring ourselves to be better than them." When I ponder the disappointments that I may have caused, it makes a lump come to my throat. It dawns on me all of the things I had planned to do and never got around to such as the call or text that I should have made to check on a friend who recently went through surgery, the sympathy card that I meant to send and never got around to, and the meal I was going to prepare for the person in need. It occurs to me that we all fall short of even our own expectations of ourselves.

When has someone treated you unfairly?
_____
_____
_____

Have you ever been accused of not being fair?
_____
_____
_____

Is life fair? Why does everyone expect it to be?
_____
_____
_____

There are three points I would like to focus on from Micah 6:8: *justice, kindness* and *humbly*.

Write the definition for the following words:
Justice:_____
_____

Kindness:_____
_____

Humbly:_____
_____

Justice

Why is it considered not fair to give the winner of the bingo game a treat and no one else? Doesn't the winner deserve a little something special since he or she won? Why do mothers and teachers hear "That isn't fair" almost weekly, if not daily?

Here's another scenario: Is it fair that one friend gets the biopsy result of benign while the other gets the results of stage 4 breast cancer? One is rejoicing, while the other is trying her best to muster all the faith she can just to stay hopeful.

Is it fair that a young life is viciously taken, leaving small children to grow up without their mother?

Why does everyone expect life to be fair? The fair only comes once a year. So hop on the roller coaster, the ups and downs that occur, and know that everything in life will not be fair or the same as your friends or family; however, if you are a Christian, you have the assurance that God is right there with you.

Do we really want to be treated fairly? If so, then we would want to be punished for all of our sins. Was it fair that Jesus was beaten, scourged, ridiculed, and died on the cross? He was perfect and without blemish. It was not fair that Jesus endured such pain, anguish, and separation from God for what I had done. What kind of justice is that? Yet He did it for me and for you.

What is the worst thing that has happened to you?
_____
_____
_____

How did God see you through that difficult time in your life?
_____
_____
_____

When bad things happen, the question arises, *Why?* Why did those terrible things happen to such a great family? They were doing all the right things. A similar question I hear is, *Why did God allow that to happen?* We have to get to the place where we simply just trust God. He knows the whole story. We only know things from our small perspective. It's in God's hands. Learn to let go and let God! As C. S. Lewis once said, "Hardships often prepare ordinary people for an extraordinary destiny." Let us live by Matthew 26:42: "Not my will, but yours be done."

Here is a poem my amazing husband wrote during a difficult season in our lives when we were searching for understanding and all we could think of was Proverbs 3:5: "Trust in the Lord with all your heart, and do not lean on your own understanding."

In God's Hands

Days come when all we want to do is cry,
Take God's hand
And give Him your every sigh,

When we are scared and confused
And don't know what to do;
Take God's hand

And He will see you through.

If your heart is broken
And the pain is more than you can bear;
Take God's hand
And He will heal your every care.

When life on earth is done
Remember, you are not alone;
Take God's hand
And He will take you home.

In God's hands,
In God's hands
Place all your burdens in God's hand

What do you need to place in God's Hands? List them below:

We are charged to "do justice" in Micah 6:8. What does that mean? What does it look like?

_____
_____
_____

Merriam-Webster defines *do justice* as "to treat or show something or someone in a way that is as good as it should be." When things of this life seem unjust, do the right thing anyway. Allow God to take care of it. Vengeance is mine, says the Lord (Romans 12:19).

Read Genesis 50:20. We see here that even Joseph's brothers felt like justice needed to be served for their mistreatment of Joseph. Forgiveness is what Joseph gave them in return. God's Word reveals to us that He indeed takes care of us. It may not always seem that way in each and every circumstance of life, but rest assured God will take care of it.

Read Amos 5:24. Fill in the missing words: "But let _____ roll down like water and righteousness like an ever-flowing stream."

JUST DIRT ON THE DRESS

Read Deuteronomy 16:19-20. What did Moses charge the Israelites to pursue?

_____
_____
_____

What are examples of not pursuing justice?

_____
_____
_____

Read Proverbs 21:2-3. What is desired by the Lord?

_____
_____
_____

Read Psalm 33:5. What does God love?

_____
_____
_____

Read 2 Peter 3:9-10. What do these verses say about our Lord?

_____
_____
_____

Read Isaiah 30:18, and then fill in the blanks: "Therefore the Lord _____ to be _____ to _____. And therefore He _____ on _____ to have _____ on _____. For the Lord is a _____ of _____. How _____ are all those who _____ for _____."

For I know my transgressions, and my sin is ever before me. Against Thee, Thee only, I have sinned, and done what is evil in Thy sight, so that Thou are justified when Thou dost speak, and blameless when Thou dost judge. (Ps. 51:3-4)

Kindness

In the fictitious story of *Cinderella*, what was it that stayed with you the most? For me, it was all about the happily ever after. The sadness and cruelty that Cinderella must have endured did not sink in until the most recent movie in 2015 was in theaters. The theme of having courage and being kind resonated with me. Is one easier than the other? We can have both!

The opposite of *kindness* is *strife*, which means quarreling or seeking superiority. What insights do you gain from the following scriptures that allow strife to be churned up?

Proverbs 30:33

Proverbs 28:5

Proverbs 28:25

Read Psalm 89:14 to see how Christians should behave.

Read Colossians 3:12 and fill in the missing words: "And so, as those who have been chosen of God, holy and beloved, put on a heart of _____, _____, _____, _____, and _____."

Presented here are ways we should and should not act as followers of Christ. When we get angry, we must get rid of that anger. Cool down. Take a deep breath before you act. Do not be arrogant but always trusting in the Lord. The earth is full of the loving kindness of the Lord. Remember to put on your heart of compassion, kindness, humility, gentleness, and patience.

Walk Humbly

We must learn to walk humbly before our Lord. His word assures us that we will not always understand everything in life. God wants our trust. In God we trust! Trust coincides with His peace. The two harmonize together like a beautiful duet.

Read Exodus 10:3 and fill in the missing words: Pharaoh refused to _____ himself before God.

What happened as a result?
_____
_____
_____

Read 1 Peter 5:5-7. What are Christians to clothe themselves with?
_____
_____
_____

Read Psalm 37:11 NASB and fill in the blanks: "But the _____ will _____ the _____ and will _____ themselves in _____ prosperity."

Read Proverbs 22:4 and fill in the blanks: "The reward of _____ and the fear of the Lord are _____, _____ and _____."

Read Matthew 23:12 and fill in the missing words: "And whoever _____ himself, shall be _____; and whoever _____ himself shall be _____."

Read James 4:6 and fill in the missing words: "But He gives a great grace. Therefore it says, 'God is opposed to the proud, but gives _____ to the humble."

How then should we live according to Philippians 2:3?
_____
_____
_____

Is it always easy to follow Philippians 2:3 when we are hurt or feel let down by others? How do you overcome it?
_____
_____
_____

Is it a coincidence that the word that follows *humble* in my *Concordance* is *humiliate*? No one ever likes to be humiliated or have an embarrassing moment in front of others. For some of us, it is just a chance we have to take to follow our destiny.

Writing is a labor of love. Being vulnerable takes tremendous courage for me. For others, it's just so easy to be real and express everything they think and feel. For an overthinker, people pleaser, and perfectionist wannabe, it's excruciating, draining, and humiliating. We have to take a chance of being humiliated in front of our peers, family, and community in order to bring glory to God. Are you willing to humble yourself before God to bring Him glory?

It isn't about my resume, as Whitney Capps said, "It's about God and what He can do." God told Moses, "Here I Am." He is there for us, we just need to pause long enough in our day to notice Him, hear Him, see Him, and listen to Him."

Read 2 Corinthians 12:21. What did Paul fear in the second letter to the Corinthians?
_____
_____
_____

Because of Jesus, we do not have to receive the justice we deserve. He saved us and set us free from the eternal consequences we deserve. As a result, we should walk humbly with God each day by allowing Him to be our Father, our guide, and our pilot. Psalm 48:14 states, "For this God is our God forever and ever; He will be our guide even to the end." Allow God to open your eyes to see how you can show kindness to the others around you. It is through our actions that we show Christ to the world around us. Do as Psalm 33:1-5 says:

> Sing for joy in the Lord, O you righteous ones; Praise is becoming to the upright. Give thanks to the Lord with the lyre; Sing praises to Him with a harp of ten strings. Sing to Him a new song; Play skillfully with a shout of joy. For the word of the Lord is upright; And all His work is done in faithfulness. He loves righteousness and justice; The earth is full of the lovingkindness of the Lord.

My song of the day: "Amazing Grace (My Chains Are Gone)" by Chris Tomlin
Your song of the day: _____

DAY 5

Justify

Who will bring a charge against God's elect? God is the one who justifies.
—Romans 8:33

Who Will Bring a Charge Against You?

Who will bring a charge against you? Satan will! He relentlessly accuses you of not being good enough and uses tactics to stall your progress and productivity. He does not always blatantly come to you with temptation. He's the master deceiver.

As I'm writing this Bible study, Satan is hard at work to stall my progress and give me doubts, insecurities, and feelings of just not being good enough or knowledgeable enough. This is true, but God is able! God is more than just good enough. He is great, mighty, capable, all-knowing, and all-powerful! Remember, "I can do ALL things through Christ who strengthens me" (Phil. 4:13)

All I have to say is, "Here I am. Send Me" (Isa. 6:8b).

God is the one who justifies each of us. He clears us, vindicates us, and makes us righteous. We are God's elect; His chosen one.

God's Elect

Read Romans 8:31-39.
Who is for us? _____
Who justifies? _____
What does *justify* mean? _____
Fill in the missing words from Romans 8:38 NIV: "For I am convinced that neither _____ nor _____, neither _____ nor _____,

neither the _____ nor the _____, nor _____ _____, neither _____ nor _____, nor _____ _____ ___ ___ _____, will be able to separate us from the love of God that is in Christ Jesus our Lord."

Read Isaiah 43:1. What does this scripture mean to you?

_____
_____
_____

Who has called us by name? _____
Read Ephesians 1:3-4. Who did God chose? _____

Radiant Bride, *you* are chosen by God. He has selected His bride.
Mark Hitchcock said this in his book *Bible Prophecy*:

Just as every wedding has certain people who participate in the ceremony, a wedding also has a schedule of events that must occur. A wedding in ancient Israel had four main steps or phases. Each phase of ancient wedding ceremonies has a spiritual parallel to the believer's relationship with Christ.

Take a look at the first phase.

The Selection of the Bride by the Father

Obviously, the first step to any marriage ceremony is the selection of a bride. In ancient Israel, the father of the bridegroom made the official selection with input, consultation, and encouragement (no doubt) from the son and his mother. Scripture declares that before God the Father created the world, He selected a bride for his beloved Son: "Long ago, even before He made the world, God loved us and chose us in Christ to be holy and without fault in His eyes." (Eph. 1:4)

For any wedding to take place, a bride must be chosen. Read the following scriptures and write down a phrase for each. Pay attention to who is chosen or called from each verse.

2 Thessalonians 2:13-15 _____
2 Timothy 1:9 _____
John 15:16 _____
Ephesians 2:8-10 _____
1 Thessalonians 1:4-5 _____

Colossians 3:12-14 _____
Matthew 22:14 _____
Who will bring a charge against you?

_____
_____
_____

There may come a time when others, even friends or family, bring a charge against you for being a Christian. It will not be easy or pleasant, but be ready with His words. Be gentle as Christ was with us.

Jot down words and scriptures that you can share with those who bring a charge against you so that you may be ready to share the good news of the gospel.

Read 2 Timothy 2:10. What are the elect charged to do?

_____
_____
_____

We are all justified because of grace through the forgiveness of sin by the death, burial, and resurrection of our Lord and Savior, Jesus Christ. He endured all things in order to give us eternal glory.

Grace

Read Romans 5:17. Because of Jesus's sacrifice for each of us, we are made justified. Christians are righteous in the sight of God because Jesus has washed away all of our sins. We have an abundance of grace through our Lord and Savior, Jesus Christ. Satan tries to tell us that we messed up today so God does not love us as much as He did yesterday when we behaved better. God is unchangeable, and His love remains the same yesterday, today, and tomorrow. It is not conditional on our actions. As R. Joyner once said,

> True grace imparts a truth that sets people free, showing them the way out of their sin, and beckoning them to higher levels of spiritual maturity. The grace of God will lead us up the mountain step by step.

Giving grace to everyone else is so much easier than giving it to myself. My own self-inflicted wounds kept me black and blue on the inside. When I made a mistake, I replayed it over and over again in my mind, beating myself up each time. I had to learn to accept the grace that was given through Jesus.

Write a note of adoration to God in the space below. Thank Him for choosing you as His Beloved and for the Grace that was shone to you as His Bride.

_____
_____
_____
_____
_____
_____

Being a Christian is not always easy—just look at Jesus's life. As we draw closer to God, sometimes the battle gets harder. Stand firm! Charges will be brought to you. Comments like, "You are really religious" (of course, spoken in a derogatory manner) or "You can take your Jesus somewhere else" (even from a friend) could set you back if you allow it, not to mention the comments you hear in your own head coming from Satan to steer you off the right path. Fight the good fight! Keep His Word hidden in your heart and be ready for the battle may get hard, but we know who ends up victorious! We know how the story ends.

Keep Psalm 101:1 in your heart: "I will sing of lovingkindness and justice, To Thee, O Lord, I will sing praises."

As we close out today's lesson, please read Romans 8:28-30. Fill in the missing words and ponder what these verses truly mean to us as Christians: "And we know that God causes all things to work together for _____ to those who are _____ according to _____ purpose. For whom He foreknew, He also predestined to become conformed to the image of His Son, that He might be the first-born among many brethren; and whom He predestined, these He also _____; and whom He _____, these He also _____; and whom He _____, these He also _____."

My song of the day: "Grace Wins" by Matthew West
Your song of the day: _____

WEEK 1 DISCUSSION

Day 1. Why did God provide a way of salvation for each of us?

Day 2. How do you become just with God?

Day 3. Suppose Jesus chose not to die for us. How would our lives be different?

Day 4. Is life fair? Why does everyone expect it to be?

Day 5. Who will bring a charge against you?

Insights to share:

WEEK 2

Dirt

DAY 1

Dig in the Dirt

*Set your **affection** on things above, not on things on the earth.*
—Colossians 3:2 (KJV, emphasis mine)

What Areas of Sin (Omission and Commission) Do You Uncover in Your Habits?

Sometimes dirt gets splattered on you all by yourself, and then there are times when dirt is splattered on you by others. It can be intentional or by mere carelessness. No matter how it gets on you, just remember that it's just dirt on the dress. Dust it off! Don't let it define you, don't let it ruin you, and, by all means, don't let it prevent you from fulfilling God's calling and purpose for your life. Shake it off! Say it away! Pray it away! Let the blood of Jesus wash it away! Just like what Beth Moore said in her book *Jesus: 90 Days with the One and Only*:

> Dirt is dirt, and we've all got it no matter where we come from. I'm not sure Christ sees one kind of dirt as dirtier than another. One thing is for sure: His blood is able to bleach any stain left by any kind of dirt.

When I was a child, I spent many hours playing outside in the dirt. I was the middle child for eight years between two brothers prior to my sister finally making her arrival. By no means was I a girly girl. Many hours would go by while I was playing in the dirt, and digging tunnels for my Hot Wheels to travel through between the roots of trees was an all-day affair.

Additionally, hiding my treasures in the dirt was one of my favorite pastimes. After some time, I would return to them and discover my pennies looked green and tarnished. It's a shame I didn't know the vinegar trick back then or I could have watched in amazement as those tarnished pennies become like new again. Jesus makes us new again but not with vinegar, water, or detergent—He made us new with His blood.

The definition of *dirt* is "a substance, such as mud or dust, that soils someone or something." Additionally, it means "loose soil or earth"; "the ground such as what is used to make a surface for a road, floor, or other area of ground." Some common synonyms as searched in the Internet are *grime, filth, soot, muck, sludge, grunge, gunge, crud, silt,* and *clay.*

In Genesis 2:7, it states that the Lord God formed man of dust. Fill in the missing words: "Then the Lord God formed man of _____ from the _____, and breathed into his nostrils the breath of life; and man became a living being."

Dust can be a noun or a verb per Google's definition:

> Dust can be a fine, dry powder consisting of tiny particles of earth or waste matter lying on the ground or on surfaces or carried in the air. The act of dusting is to remove the dust from the surface of (something) by wiping or brushing it.

Dirt was splattered on me at a very young age. I didn't dust it off. I covered it with guilt and shame. I felt like it was my fault—that somehow, I should have known to say no. But I didn't at eight years old. Inappropriate touching left me covered in shame, guilt, and an awkwardness that I could not describe at that time. The treasure of my innocence was taken, stolen, and replaced with dirt and shame. It dressed me in shame and made me feel like less of a person. It disgusted me, and I was disgusted in myself.

As time went on, I grew a self-defeated attitude. I felt dingier and dingier. No shine, no sparkle. People I trusted let me down. As a result, I did not trust people for a long time. I put up a wall around me so as not to be hurt again. Sure, on the outside, everything looked fine. I got along well with others, made good grades in school, played softball, followed the rules, tried to do what's right, but still never felt good enough. The dirt I carried around with me was shame, and the longer I went without removing it, the worse it felt. It was like a splinter festering for over thirty years. Finally, it became more than I could bear.

The book *The Courage to Heal: A Guide for Women Survivors of Child Sexual Abuse* tells us this:

> Before you can let go of shame, you have to recognize it, name it, and hold it out in the light of day. When you keep shame a secret, it gains power of you. Admitting shame is a first step in deflating its power.

Read Psalm 44:21. What does God know?

_____
_____
_____

What are your secrets of the heart?

_____
_____
_____

Read Ecclesiastes 12:13-14. What are we to do as Christians?

_____
_____
_____

What will God bring to judgment?

_____
_____
_____

Read Matthew 13:44. What is the meaning of the Parable of the Hidden Treasure? What is the treasure?

_____
_____
_____

In this week's lesson, let's dig in to find areas of weaknesses and areas of sin in our lives in order to uncover the treasure that awaits. That treasure is Jesus and his saving grace.

Is there a cycle of sins or temptations that keep popping up?

_____
_____
_____

Remember, Satan tries to get you to see only the dirt, the sins, and the bad things. We are going to mess things up. Accept it and know that God forgives you. Learn from it and try your best not to get into a cycle of the same sins. It is just dirt on the dress; allow Jesus to clean it up for you. When Jesus cleans, He cleans it perfectly.

Do you ever have thoughts where you think, *Where in the world did that come from?* It can even happen while reading scripture or, at least, it has for me. I can have whole scenarios going on in my mind while my eyes continue to read an entire page of scriptures. I have to stop and think, *What in the world just happened? What did I read?*

Then I have to remind Satan to get behind me while I'm trying to draw closer to God: "For my thoughts are not your thoughts and my ways are not your ways" (Isa. 55:8). I hold onto the promise in James 4:7: "Therefore submit to God. Resist the devil and he will flee from you. Draw near to God and He will draw near to you." I no longer want to be double-minded because God wants us to "Cleanse your hands, you sinners; and purify your hearts, you double-minded" (James 4:8).

What is your go-to scripture to help you resist the sins that are your greatest temptations?

_____
_____
_____

I didn't realize I was so broken until all of the cracks came together. All my life, I have worried about what others thought of me because I thought the worst of me. I placed name tags of Shame, Regret, and Not Good Enough on my dress. I don't want to be remembered for being a dirty girl; the molested child; or the sweet, quiet one. Rather, I want to be known as someone who devoted her life to the glory of God and helped others along the way. Ultimately, it does not matter what everyone else thinks of me. What God thinks of me is all that matters!

Writing letters, even to yourself, is therapeutic. I wrote a letter to myself similar to this one and sent it up on a balloon. It was like I was releasing those feelings up to heaven.

Fill in your name and add to this letter things that pertain to your life or write a completely different letter to yourself to fit your circumstances.

Dear _____,

> You need to be kind to yourself! You are not the experiences you have gone through. You are stronger because of them—not weaker! You are amazing! A precious child of God is what you are! God's treasure! His gem! Look at what all you've accomplished. Focus on how you felt after reaching each goal. Focus on the positives. You have got to stop beating yourself up! You are black and blue on the inside from your own

self-inflicted wounds. It is time to share some of that love you give others with yourself.

See yourself as God sees you: a child of God, fearfully and wonderfully made. You were made in His image, by His design. Say to yourself, "I am who I was designed to be." Accept yourself just as you are! It is also time to forgive yourself! Forgive yourself for your past mistakes. Forgive others who have thrown dirt on you! Let that anchor go! You have blossomed into a beautiful creature. Do not worry about what others think about you. What matters is what God thinks about you, and He loves you unconditionally! Now, you have some time to make up. Get busy loving you so you can love others better!

Love,

_____

Deep study of God's word and reflection is needed in order to keep the dirt and sin from reoccurring as is written in the Bible: "Therefore, having these promises, beloved, let us cleanse ourselves from all defilement of flesh and spirit, perfecting holiness in the fear of God" (2 Cor. 7:1). Dig away at the dirt to find the treasure. It is there! Each of us is valuable to God. We have been bought with a price—Jesus's life (1 Cor. 6:20). Remember, there is a day coming when there will be an end to all of the sin and temptations.

Read Psalm 119:11. Fill in the missing words: "Thy _____ I have _____ in my _____, that I may not sin against Thee.

Read Matthew 6:19-21. Fill in the missing words. "Do not lay up for yourselves _____ upon earth, where moth and rust destroy, and where thieves break in and steal. But lay up for yourselves _____ in _____, where neither moth nor rust destroys, and where thieves do not break in or steal; for where your _____ is, there will your _____ be also."

What does splatter mean?
_____
_____
_____

Splatter good deeds in your community. Do them in secret and receive your treasure in Heaven for the good you splatter around our world.

What will you splatter around your community this week?

_____
_____
_____

Hidden Treasures to be Found

Read the John 1:16; Colossians 2:3; Proverbs 2:1-10; Isaiah 1:18; and Psalm 51:6 and write down hidden treasures to be found in God's Word:

1. _____

2. _____

3. _____

4. _____

5. _____

God's Word is a plethora of treasures! Just some of the treasures from the above verses are acceptance or reconciliation, humility, citizenship/eternal life, saving grace, purity, sins made as white as snow, wisdom, and knowledge.

Now, it is your turn. Go on a treasure hunt. Just open your Bible.

Put your finger on a verse and write it down. Make it your verse of the day.
_____

Which verse or verses are your greatest treasures?
_____
_____
_____

What treasures have you found in God's Word?
_____
_____
_____

Read Psalm 119:11 and Luke 2:19. What are the similarities between these two verses?

_____
_____
_____

One day while writing this chapter, my treasure hunt discovered this verse: "And immediately, when the entire crowd saw Him, they were amazed, and began running up to greet Him" (Mark 9:15). Be amazed, Radiant Bride, by Jesus and run to greet your beloved!

Read Philippians 3:20-21. Where is our citizenship as Christians?

_____
_____
_____

How will your body be transformed from your humble state to the body of His glory?

_____
_____
_____

How do you picture yourself dressed in His Glory?

_____
_____
_____

Read Colossians 1:19-22. How does Jesus reconcile us and present us to our Heavenly Father?

_____
_____
_____

Read Colossians 3:1-4. Who is our life? _____
Who will be revealed with Jesus in Glory? _____

On my wedding day, I looked down, and there they were—two brown spots on the front of my wedding gown. *Well, isn't that symbolic*, I thought. Those two spots represented the two people who hurt me the most. How I wanted to feel pure, blameless, and spotless on my special day, but that was taken from me! My precious innocence was taken like a pair of the most expensive diamonds stolen in the dead of night. It forever changed me, but I refuse to let the story end there. I will allow God to change me in order to glorify Him with my life.

There came a time when I had to make a decision, whether to share my dirt or not. Would I have the courage to expose the dirt to the world? Did I want to be that vulnerable? Could I handle the naysayers? Then, I realized that I was seeking the approval of many rather than the approval of the only one who matters—God.

Do not be silent about your trials and struggles. Do not let it eat you from the inside out or try to shovel food on top of it. That's what I did. It doesn't work. The only thing that heals is the healing word of God and His presence. He alone transforms us from the inside out! If you remain silent, where is your testimony? It gets buried along with you when your time on earth is over. You are the only one who knows your story. Share your story so others can know how God worked in your life.

Many women have had to face far greater trials and harsher things than I did. Rape, sex trafficking, physical abuse, emotional abuse, and the like are all by far some of the worst trials of life. My trial was minimal in comparison, but how we respond to the trial makes all the difference in the world. Are we going to play the part of the victim or the victor? I have played the part of the victim for far too long. I'm ready for a little victory in Jesus.

One of my favorite hymns is "Victory in Jesus." One of the lines says, "O victory in Jesus, my Savior forever! He sought me and bought me with His redeeming blood; He loved me ere I knew Him, and all my love is due Him—He plunged me to victory beneath the cleansing flood!" You no longer have to think of yourself as the dirty girl for you are a precious child of God, fearfully and wonderfully made by the Creator of everything beautiful. You are so loved, Radiant Bride, and He will plunge you to victory beneath His cleansing blood!

As we close out today's lesson, I'd like to leave you with the verse from Psalm 103:13-14: "Just as a father has compassion on His children, so the Lord has compassion on those who fear Him. For He Himself knows our frame; He is mindful that we are but dust."

Remember to set your mind on things above and not on the things of this earth. Find the hidden treasure found only in scriptures. Our Heavenly Father knows that we are but dust and we will dirty up our dress. Allow the dirt on the dress to be cleaned by the blood of Jesus which covers our sins and makes us as white as snow. What is it about snow? Its beauty is beyond compare. It can fall on a pile of heap yet still be the most beautiful thing you ever did see. It covers the dirt and gives it a blanket of purity.

That is what the blood of Jesus does for us. It makes us as white as snow—pure, spotless, and beautiful. For those who fear the Lord, He will cover up our dirt with the blood of Jesus which bleaches out all our iniquities and makes us clean! "There's nothing too dirty, that you can't make worthy. You wash me in mercy, I am clean … Washed in the blood, of your sacrifice. Your blood flowed red, and made me white. My dirty rags are purified, I am clean," the song "Clean!" by Natalie Grant goes. His compassion is beyond measure for each of us. Remember Psalm 96:1-2: "Sing to the Lord a new song; Sing to the Lord, all the earth. Sing to the Lord, bless His name; Proclaim good tidings of His salvation from day to day."

    My song of the day: "Clean!" by Natalie Grant
    Your song of the day: _____

DAY 2

Iniquity to Influence

Wash me thoroughly from my iniquity, and cleanse me from my sin.
—Psalm 51:2

How Can You Turn Your Iniquity into a Positive Influence on Others' Lives?

Children are precious, a true gift from God. Part of what makes them special is their pure innocence. They haven't been tainted by this dark world.

The term *innocence* in *Merriam-Webster* means "a lack of guilt with respect to any kind of crime or other wrong act." It also means "a lack of experience with the world and with the bad things in it."

Big sins, little sins—sin is sin. I can remember one of my first sins, if not the first one. When I was six years old, I walked out of a local store with a tube of lip balm. I do not recall what prompted me to take it, but I remember lying to my mom later about where I got it. One sin led to another. Before we know it, innocence turns into iniquity. I'm glad there is not a running tally of the sins I commit like a pedometer keeping up with the steps I have taken in a day.

This chapter will take us through several important *I* words. We will take a look at how quickly innocence can become iniquity, and then through our iniquity, we gain insight through the study of God's word, which ultimately leads us to having a positive influence on the world for God's glory. Through Jesus's righteousness, our innocence is renewed.

Genesis 2:22-23 states,

> And the Lord God fashioned into a woman the rib which He had taken from the man, and brought her to the man. And the man said,

this is now bone of my bones, and flesh of my flesh; she shall be called Woman, because she was taken out of man.

Have you ever noticed how quickly the fall of man occurs in scriptures? We do not know the distance of time between the creation of man and woman and the first sin. Time is not of importance for a day is like a thousand years and a thousand years is like a day (2 Pet. 3:8). In Genesis 2:23, we read that God created woman from Adam's rib. Just three verses later, we read about the temptation of man, and by Genesis 3:6, we are reading about the fall of man. No indication of time is given for us, but do you ever wonder how quickly it could have occurred?

Thankfully, the story doesn't end there. All we have to do is acknowledge our sins to God, and He is faithful to forgive us (Ps. 32:5).

Fill in the missing word from Psalm 51:2: "Wash me thoroughly from my _____, and cleanse me from my sin."

Go just a few verses further and fill in the missing words from Psalm 51:9: "Hide Thy face from my _____, and _____ out all my _____."

Read Proverbs 29:6 and complete the blanks: "By _____ an evil man is _____, but the _____ _____ and _____."

Iniquity

Write the key word or phrase from each of the following verses:
    Psalm 25:11 _____
    Psalm 32:1-2; 5 _____
    Psalm 51:9 _____
    Psalm 103:8; 12 _____
    Isaiah 53:5 _____
    Ezekiel 18:30-32 _____
    James 3:6 _____

Read Jeremiah 33:8-11 What does God promise to cleanse the people from? _____

What will the voices of bride and bridegroom say in Jeremiah 33:11 as they bring thank offerings to the house of the Lord? (Fill in the blanks.) "Give _____ to the _____ _____, for the _____ is _____; His _____ endures _____."

Read 1 John 1:7-9. How are we to walk?

_____
_____
_____

Iniquity is darkness; influence is light. Strive to walk in the light of Jesus. Regardless of our iniquity, the first of many sins we commit or the last, Jesus gives us a Robe of Righteousness.

Robe of Righteousness

Because of Jesus
It's all because of Jesus
Given a Robe of Righteousness
His sacrifice
His blood
His Life
Given for me
To cleanse
Every sin and stain

Unaware of what I was doing
Or just didn't care
They are all washed away
Washed away
And replaced with
A Robe of Righteousness

Pure white & without blemish
A Robe of Righteousness
Radiant, glowing, pure and free
Forgiven of all Iniquity

How can you turn your iniquity or shortcomings around to be an example in order to have a positive influence on the lives of others?

_____
_____
_____

Christians strive to be a positive influence on others, not to earn his or her salvation but in order to win lost souls to Jesus, to encourage one another, and to build each other up and not cause anyone to stumble.

Insight: Growth in Christ

Let's dissect two passages of scripture in order to gain insight on how we can be a positive influence on others.

Read 2 Peter 1:3-11. Give examples of how to demonstrate the following attributes:

Escape corruption of this world: _____
_____

Apply diligence: _____
_____

Moral excellence: _____
_____

Gain knowledge: _____
_____

Self-control: _____
_____

Perseverance: _____
_____

Godliness: _____
_____

Brotherly kindness: _____
_____

Love: _____
_____

Read Philippians 4:8. Keep your mind on the following. Write at least one example of each attribute:
True:
Honorable:
Right:
Pure:
Lovely:
Good repute:
Excellence:
Worthy of praise:

Influence

Read 2 Corinthians 12:7-10. What have we been given in order to be an influence in the world?

_____
_____
_____

Read John 1:6-9. What was John referred to as in these verses?

_____
_____
_____

Read John 8:12-14. What did Jesus say in verse 12?

_____
_____
_____

What are we promised to have if we follow Jesus?

_____
_____
_____

Think of your witness as the lights of the candelabras at a wedding. Brides go to great length to have all of the accessories just right for their wedding, and candles are a big part of that. You be the light in this dark world. Share the light of Jesus with all you come in contact with—whether at the grocery store, work, or throughout the community you live in. Be the light for Jesus!

Read Matthew 10:14. What are we to do if others do not want to hear about the saving grace of Jesus?

_____
_____
_____

What did Jesus promise his disciples in Matthew 10:19-20? Do you think the same is true for you? Will the Holy Spirit give you the words to say?

_____
_____
_____
_____

Many times, my prayer to God is to give me the words to say because I know I cannot do it on my own. Have you ever had a brain freeze in the middle of a large group? It isn't pretty.

Read Proverbs 12:26. What should the righteous choose carefully?

_____
_____
_____

Read Colossians 1:9-14. In what ways do you live a life worthy of the Lord and please Him in every way?

_____
_____
_____

Read Philippians 2:14-16. If you become children of God, what will you shine like?

_____
_____
_____

Read Proverbs 13:9. How does the light of the righteous shine?

_____
_____
_____

When we allow God to work with the iniquities from our past, we are not only cleansed from them with the blood of Jesus, but we also have a testimony. Our lives can influence others to come to know Jesus as Lord and Savior. As Christians, we never claim to be perfect. We are sinners saved by grace, trying to spread His light into this dark world one candlestick at a time.

"My Sins Are Blotted Out, I Know!" is an old hymn that goes like this:

> What a wondrous message in God's Word! My Sins are blotted out, I know! If I trust in His redeeming blood, my sins are blotted out, I know! My sins are blotted out, I know! My sins are blotted out, I know! They are buried in the depths of the deepest sea; my sins are blotted out, I know! (*Great Hymns of the Faith*, 200)

As we close today's lesson and prepare for tomorrow's lesson, I would like to bring to your attention Titus 3:5-6:

> He saved us, not on the basis of deeds which we have done in righteousness, but according to His mercy, by the washing of regeneration and renewing by the Holy Spirit, whom He poured out upon us richly through Jesus Christ our Savior.

Sometimes, our iniquity can be the very thing that can lead another one to Christ. When we share what God has done for us after we repent from our iniquity, then we can make a positive influence on the lives of those around us as well as this world we are merely passing through. Take Psalm 71:22-23 to heart:

> I will also praise Thee with a harp, Even Thy truth, O my God; To thee I will sing praises with the lyre, O Thou Holy One of Israel. My lips will shout for joy when I sing praises to Thee; and my soul, which Thou hast redeemed. My tongue also will utter Thy righteousness all day long.

My song of the day: "Unchangeable" by Matthew West
Your song of the day: _____

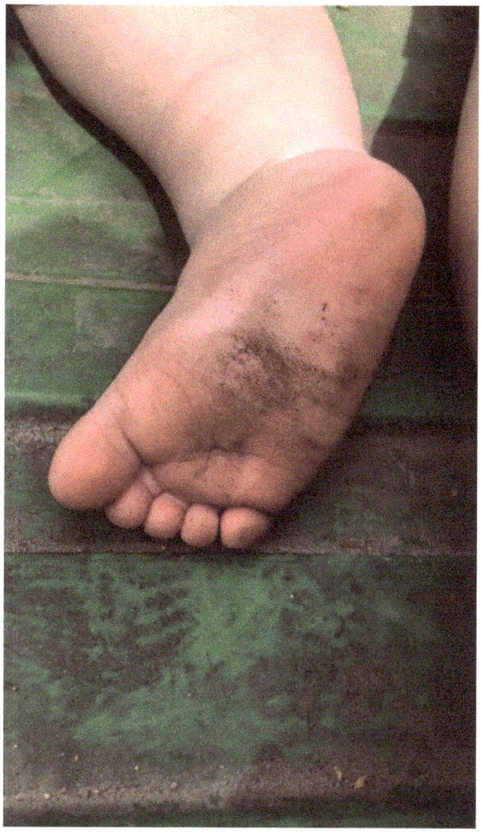

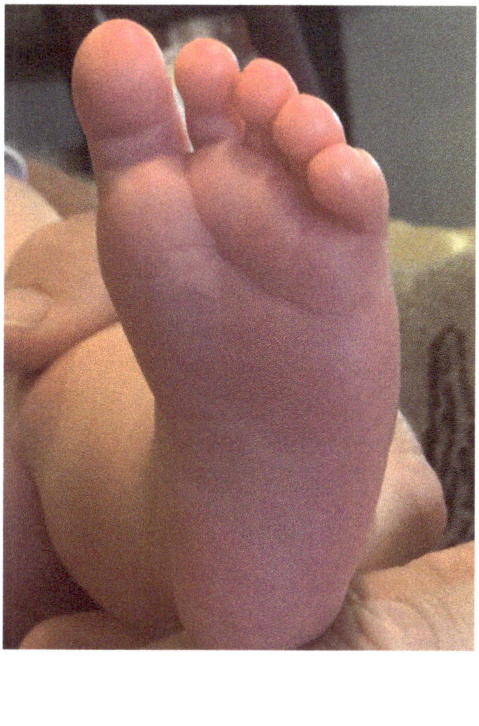

DAY 3

Renew

Create in me a clean heart, O God, and renew a steadfast spirit within me.
—Psalm 51:10

How Does God See Us through the Saving Grace of Jesus?

My husband, Jera, gets a great deal of enjoyment out of restoring old cars. It is really quite fascinating to see how he transforms an old, beat-up car or truck into looking brand-new with shiny paint, new interior, a spotless engine, perfect door panels, clean carpeting, a flawless dash, and, of course, new lights and gauges. Hours upon hours are spent polishing chrome until it meets his satisfaction.

I love that Jera has found one of his new favorites, a 1939 Chevy Truck. We call this rat rod "Shake." It is patina with a clear coat. It is nature's way of painting it. In other words, it looks like rust with a shiny coat. What a great reminder that we are fine just the way we are! When we put on the clear coat of Christ, we become shiny and new. We shine for His glory!

My maiden name is New. My desire for many years was to be a New Gina. I was tired of not measuring up to my own standards for myself, not being just like so and so and carrying that dingy coat of shame around everywhere that I went. Feeling pure, spotless, and being good enough were what I was seeking. Oh, how I wanted to be brand-new!

Every year, I would make resolutions to try to become a better version of myself, only to have given up by the end of January. After years of trying to change myself and failing time and time again, I decided just to put it in the hands of God and allow Him to change me as He desired. I wasn't going to tell God that He made me wrong; too quiet, too fat, and not good enough. Now, I resolve to be a child of God, the clay in the Potter's hand, and the Bride of Christ. As written in Psalm 139:14: "I will give thanks to You, for I am fearfully and wonderfully made; wonderful are your works, and my soul knows it very well."

Have you ever noticed you begin to act a certain way when you are around one friend compared to another? You begin to take on some of their mannerisms or expressions. Likewise, when we stay in God's word and commune with Him through prayer, we become more like Him.

We were all created in the image of God; however, the more you fellowship with Him, you become polished—if you will—into a mirrored image of God. When you allow God to work in your life, you continue to transform into something more beautiful. His beautiful spirit within us begins to shine forth for all to see.

Define *renew*:_____
_____

Define *steadfast*: _____
_____

Read Psalm 51:12. What should we ask God to restore in us?
_____
_____
_____

Read Psalm 103:1-5, and then fill in the missing words:

Bless the Lord, O my soul; and all that is within me, bless His holy name. Bless the Lord, O my soul, and forget none of His _____;
Who _____;
Who_____;
Who_____;
Who _____
_____;Who_____
_____;
So that your youth is _____ like the eagle.

What do the following scriptures speak to you about being renewed?

Lamentations 5:21
_____
_____
_____

Romans 12:2

_____
_____
_____

2 Corinthians 3:18

_____
_____
_____

2 Corinthians 4:16

_____
_____
_____

2 Corinthians 5:17

_____
_____
_____

Colossians 3:10-11

_____
_____
_____

What is a common word throughout these scriptures? _____

Your heart is at the center of all renewal and transformation.

Read Psalm 139:23-24. What are these verses calling out to God to do?

_____
_____
_____

What do the following scriptures speak to you about being steadfast?

Job 11:15

_____
_____
_____

Psalm 57:7

_____
_____
_____

Psalm 112:7

_____
_____
_____

1 Corinthians 15:58

_____
_____
_____

2 Thessalonians 3:5

_____
_____
_____

2 Peter 1:1-14

_____
_____
_____

I just love butterflies! They represent transformation, which is a great reminder of my own transformation that God has made through me. This year, I have noticed more white butterflies than ever before. They are called cabbage white and are the most common butterfly. According to fcps.edu,

> They are mostly white with black markings and spots on the top of their wings. Males and females can be told apart by their wing spots. Males only have one spot on each wing, while females have two.

The spots are unnoticeable as the butterflies flutter by. You only see the pure white wings, which is just how God sees us when we accept His free gift of salvation. We no longer have blots, spots, or blemishes.

When I researched the cabbage white butterfly and discovered that there were spots on their wings, it reminded me of my wedding gown. There were two spots on my otherwise perfectly white and gorgeous gown. I, unfortunately, was focused on two things that were wrong and not paying attention to the ninety-eight wonderful things that were so right on my wedding day.

When was a time that you noticed only the things that were wrong instead of the things that were right?

_____
_____
_____

How does God see us through the saving grace of Jesus?

_____
_____
_____

Like a butterfly goes through metamorphosis, Christians are transformed into a new creation because of the grace of Jesus and His act of love and obedience. Many have described the Christian faith as growing from infancy to full maturity; however, I would like to make the analogy with the life cycle of a butterfly. Focus now on your spiritual journey.

- *Egg.* Are you like an egg…just hanging around?
- *Larva—caterpillar.* Are you like a caterpillar…eating up scriptures which is your nourishment and growing day by day?
- *Pupa/cocoon.* Perhaps you are in a cocoon being transformed from the inside out while you be still and know that He is God. Sometimes, you may not see progress right away, but each day you're changing and growing to become the Christian who's free in Christ and becoming what God desires of you. Deny yourself in this stage. Be willing to give up the old self, your plans, your desires and be willing to take on God's new self for you, His plans and desires for your life. Here I am, Lord…Send Me.
- *Butterfly.* Are you flying freely as God's beautiful creation? Are you enjoying the sweet nectar of life that God has blessed you with? Are you thankful for the sweet aroma of flowers?

Overwhelmingly, cultural myth and lore honor the butterfly as a symbol of transformation because of its impressive process of metamorphosis. From egg, to larvae (caterpillar, to pupa (the chrysalis or cocoon) and from the cocoon the butterfly emerges in her unfurling glory. What a massive amount of transition this tiny creature undergoes. Consider for a moment the kind of energy this expends. I daresay if a human were to go through this kind of change we'd freak out! Imagine the whole of your life changing to such an extreme you are unrecognizable at the end of the transformation. Mind you, this change takes place in a short span of about a month too (that's how long the butterfly life cycle is). Herein lies the deepest symbolic lesson of the butterfly. She asks us to accept the changes in our lives as casually as she does. The butterfly unquestioningly embraces the chances of her environment and her body. This unwavering acceptance of her metamorphosis is also symbolic of faith. Here the butterfly beckons us to keep our faith as we undergo transitions in our lives. She understands that our toiling, fretting and anger are useless against the turning tides of nature—she asks us to recognize the same.

Christianity considers the butterfly as a symbol for the soul. To wit, the butterfly is depicted on ancient Christian tombs, as Christ has been illustrated holding a butterfly in Christian art. It's connection with the soul is rather fitting. We are all on a long journey of the soul. On this journey we encounter endless turns, shifts, and conditions that cause us to morph into ever-finer beings. At our soul-journey's end we are inevitably changed—not at all the same as when we started on the path. To take this analogy a step further, we can look again to the grace and eloquence of the butterfly and realize that our journey is our only guarantee. Our responsibility to make our way in faith, accept the change that comes, and emerge from our transitions as brilliantly as the butterfly. (Life Is an Adventure, Susan Kay Richardet)

How are the life changing stages of a butterfly similar to your own?
_____
_____
_____

Are you still crawling around looking for nourishment? Have you begun your transformation by being still and meditating on God's word? Are you ready to fly in the freedom that Christ provides?

Read Colossians 3:1-17 and Ephesians 4:23-29, and then complete the following chart comparing your old self with your new self in Christ:

Old Self   New Self

Perhaps, you put some of the same examples under the old self such as falsehood, sinner, anger, bitterness, wrath, clamor, malice, thief, and unwholesome words. These things only give the devil an opportunity to undo all of the wonderful things you have done for God's Kingdom.

Let's put on the new self! Let us be tenderhearted, filled with the Holy Spirit, kind, encouraging, giving, and forgiving. Be determined to demonstrate the likeness of God as one created in righteousness, with holiness of truth, renewed in the spirit, and as a laborer of good. Steal no longer. Share with those in need. Speak truth and do not give the devil an opportunity.

Sing this song with me:

Renew

Like a butterfly goes through
a metamorphosis,
I, too, have begun
a transformation.

I'm renewed,
changed by the blood of the Christ,
renewed by His love.

Through God's Word,
He renews my mind,
thinking more of you,
changing me through and through,
putting you first in my life,
no other idols.

Receive it!
Don't run from it!
Repent and rest in your salvation!
He's there for every snare and pitfall,
always there,
Renewing our hearts, our minds, our souls.

He put a new song in my heart,
a hymn of praise to our God.
I put my trust in the Lord;

He set me free,
resurrected a new me

New birth,
new breath,
a new day,
He alone gave me a firm place to stand.

It's never too late to make a brand-new start
to your life.
I've got my wings;
I'm ready to fly!

Ponder Titus 3:5-7 as we conclude the lesson today.

God is restoring us from our rusty, sinful selves into shiny new creations. He put a new song in my heart, a hymn of praise to our God. Renew your focus, mind, and thinking. Don't try to do it all on your own. God will transform you, but first you must give Him permission. Allow Him to do the work in you! Be transformed! Read Psalm 149:1: "Praise the Lord! Sing to the Lord a new song, And His praise in the congregation of the godly ones."

My song of the day: "Made New" by Lincoln Brewster
Your song of the day: _____

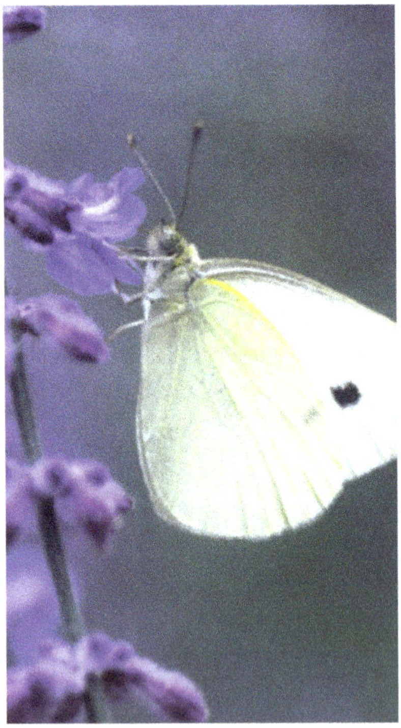

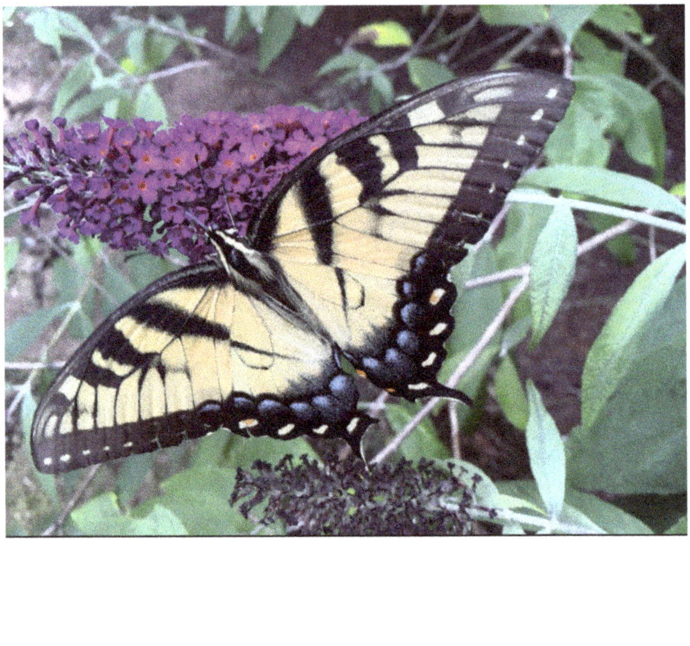

DAY 4

Tree of Life

> *She (wisdom) is a tree of life to those who take hold of her. And happy are all who hold her fast.*
> —Proverbs 3:18

How Do You Take Hold of Your Part of the Tree of Life?

One of my favorite places to go while growing up was the tree house our dad built for us in the backyard overlooking the vegetable garden. With a fireman-like pole to slide down, we could make a quick escape back to the nearby swing set. This was my happy place, my thinking place. How I loved to have time to explore and ponder! Ironically, it would also be the first place I would practice teaching with the chalkboard and little table and chair set inside. My favorite thing to do was to climb up on the rail to the shingled roof and cross over to the other side of the treehouse to the thickest part of the tree branch that created a natural seat for me. My legs would dangle loosely as I swung them back and forth, looking out at the beauty surrounding me and taking in the scent of the honeysuckle bush.

The living tree was the foundation for the dead tree that was chopped down and made into boards in order to create the treehouse. In order for the treehouse to even be in existence, something had to die. Likewise, for us to have eternal life, Jesus had to die. He hung on a tree turned into a cross for each of us. We in turn must die to ourselves, our wants, and desires and learn what it is God wants us to do daily.

Read Genesis 1:11-12. What did God see that was good?

_____
_____
_____

Read Genesis 2:9. What were in the middle of the Garden of Eden?

_____
_____
_____

The first home for the first man and woman was a garden—the Garden of Eden. They were living in a beautiful place and given a commandment: not to eat from the tree of knowledge of good and evil.

Read Genesis 2:15-17. Which tree were Adam and Eve not to eat from? Which trees could they have eaten from?

_____
_____
_____

Read Genesis 3:6. How was the fruit of the tree described?

_____
_____
_____

Not only was the fruit desirable for how it would taste, it was desirable for the wisdom it would provide. The serpent representing Satan stated, "Your eyes will be opened, and you will be like God, knowing good and evil."

Read Genesis 3:8. What did Adam and Eve hide themselves behind after eating from the forbidden fruit? _____

God's word states, "She (wisdom) is a tree of life to those who take hold of her. And happy are all who hold her fast" (Prov. 3:18).

Why is wisdom considered a tree of life?

_____
_____
_____

Wisdom is considered *a* tree of life, not *the* tree of life. Take hold of wisdom and never let go.

Beginning of Wisdom

Read Proverbs 1:7. What do fools despise?
_____
_____
_____

What is the beginning of knowledge?
_____
_____
_____

The Bible states, "The beginning of wisdom is: Acquire wisdom. And with all your acquiring, get understanding" (Prov. 4:7). That means, we, as God's children, are to put forth effort in acquiring wisdom and knowledge of our Lord through His Word that He provides for us. It is just as pertinent to us today as the day it was scribed on the scrolls. 1 Peter 1:25 says, "But the word of the Lord endures forever."

Read Jeremiah 17:7-8. Who is blessed? _____
What is a man who trusts in the Lord compared to?
_____
_____
_____

Extend your root toward the stream. Jesus offers living water. He offers it to you. Take it—extend your arms and take it!

What two synonyms are used in this passage that represent what those who trust in the Lord do not have?
_____
_____
_____

Read Luke 2:52 and fill in the missing words: "_____ kept _____ in _____ and stature and in favor with _____ and man."

Remember: "Jesus is the way, the truth and the life" (John 14:6).

Read Matthew 7:14 and fill in the missing words: "For the gate is _____ and the way is _____ that leads to _____ and few are these who find it."

Read Luke 8:10-15, the Parable of the Sower. According to verse 15, how do Christians produce a good crop?

_____
_____
_____

Read Psalm 119:9-11. How can you stay on the "path of purity"?

_____
_____
_____

Benefits of Wisdom

What are the benefits of wisdom as promised in Proverbs 3:1-26?

_____
_____
_____
_____
_____
_____

Fill in the blanks for the benefits of wisdom found in Proverbs 3:1-26:

1. Length of _____ and _____ of life
2. P_____
3. He will make your paths _____
4. _____ to your body
5. _____ to your bones
6. Barns will be _____ with _____
7. Vats will _____ with _____ _____
8. Profit better than _____ and _____ _____
9. More precious than _____
10. Riches and _____
11. _____ Ways

12. Paths are _____
13. Tree of _____
14. H_____
15. U_____
16. Deeps are _____ _____
17. Skies drip with _____
18. _____ to your _____
19. _____ to your neck
20. Walk _____
21. Foot _____ _____ stumble
22. Will not be _____
23. _____ Sleep
24. _____ _____ of sudden fear or the wicked
25. Confidence in the _____
26. Foot _____ _____ not be caught

What is wisdom worth more than?
_____
_____
_____

Even Jesus, God's only son, put forth great effort to gain wisdom. Read Luke 2:52.

Strength of Wisdom

Read Ephesians 3:16-21. Summarize these verses into a personal statement to yourself.
_____
_____
_____

What are we to do? Press on to maturity, wisdom, and understanding. Underline the key words for you in Hebrews 6:1 and Hebrews 6:7-8:

Therefore, leaving the elementary teaching about the Christ, let us press on to maturity, not laying again a foundation of repentance from dead works and of faith toward God.

For ground that drinks the rain which often falls upon it and brings forth vegetation useful to those for whose sake it is also tilled, receives a blessing from God; but if it yields thorns and thistles, it is worthless and close to being cursed, and it ends up being burned.

Read Revelation 2:7. How do you take hold of your part of the tree of life?
_____
_____
_____

Take hold of the tree of life. Take hold and never let go of your part of the tree of life. May your name be forever written in the Lamb's book of life. I think it is just fine to imagine your name carved in a tree with a heart around it. Be in love with the Lord.

HOLD ON TO YOUR PART OF THE TREE OF LIFE
HE
OFFERS
LOVE
DELIVERANCE

OVERFLOWING JOY
NEW LIFE

Read Isaiah 55:12. How are the trees of the fields described in this verse?
_____
_____
_____

Have you ever noticed leaves when the wind is blowing? At times, you can see leaves that appear to be waving at you. A smile immediately goes on my face, and I think about what a wonderful sense of humor our Lord has. I think about Colossians 3:16:

Let the word of Christ richly dwell within you, with all wisdom teaching and admonishing one another with psalms and hymns and spiritual songs, singing with thankfulness in your hearts to God.

Root

Sometimes, it's the little things that can trip us up and not the big tree roots or rocks of life that get us as stumbling blocks. We have to trap those thoughts and temptations that try to creep in by recognizing it for what it is and silencing it with prayer. Be rooted in Christ to keep from stumbling.

Unfortunately, there was a period of time when I was rooted in my family, not in God. When my children grew up and began their venture in the world of college and marriage, I was lost, confused, and unsure of who I was anymore. Now that I strive to truly make God first place in my life, I am whole again, filled with joy, and at peace with my life and circumstances.

From the dirt brings forth fruit; without dirt, there would be no flowers or trees.

Read Matthew 13:1-9. How do you ensure that the word of God is found on good soil so that it produces a crop?

_____
_____
_____

Read Revelation 22:16: "I, Jesus, have sent My angel to testify to you these things for the churches, I am the root and the offspring of David, the bright morning star." Who is the root?

_____

Be grounded in the root of Jesus! Stand firm in the good soil of His word in order to not stumble, and then you will produce a good crop for His glory. Don't allow it to be carried away with the birds, scorched and withered by the sun, or choked out by thorns and thistles—produce a hundred, sixty, or thirty times what was sown.

Bears No Fruit

Don't be like the tree that bears no fruit in Hebrews 6:7:

> For ground that drinks the rain which often falls upon it and brings forth vegetation useful to those for whose sake it is also tilled, receives a blessing from God; but if it yields thorns and thistles, it is worthless and close to being cursed, and it ends up being burned.

Read Matthew 3:10. What happens to the tree that bears no fruit?

_____
_____
_____

Read Matthew 7:17-20. What does a bad tree bear? What is cut down and thrown into the fire?

_____
_____
_____

Read Jude 12-13. How are ungodly people described in these verses?

_____
_____
_____

Tend to the Tree

Plant seeds of faith. Have you planted your mustard seeds yet?

Read Matthew 13:31. How is a mustard seed like the kingdom of heaven?

_____
_____
_____

Read Proverbs 27:18. Who will be honored?

_____
_____
_____

Read 1 Corinthians 3:6-9 and fill in the missing words: Christians are to _____ and _____, but it is God who allows it to _____.
How are Christians described in these verses? _____
Read Luke 19:4. What is made evident about Zacchaeus in this verse?

_____
_____
_____

He climbed up into a sycamore tree for the Lord he wanted to see. Zacchaeus had a longing and hope to see the Lord.

Read Proverbs 13:12. According to this verse, what is a tree of life?
_____
_____
_____

Fruit

Read Matthew 12:33-37. When good is stored up in someone, what is the result? How is good stored up in someone?
_____
_____
_____

Read Psalm 92:12. How will the righteous flourish?
_____
_____
_____

Read the following passages and write down the description given for the trees mentioned in each:
    Psalm 104:16 _____
    Psalm 52:8 _____
    Proverbs 11:30 _____

Read Revelation 2:7. Who will be given the right to eat from the tree of life?
_____
_____
_____

Wisdom of God

Read 1 Corinthians 2:5 and fill in the missing words: "I will not let my faith rest on the _____ of _____, but on the _____ of _____."

Read 1 Corinthians 3:18-23. What kind of wisdom is foolishness in the sight of God?

_____
_____
_____

Read Psalm 119:45. When we seek after God's precepts, how will we walk? What does walking at liberty look like?

_____
_____
_____

The beginning of wisdom is fear of the Lord. When we regard the Lord above everything else, we begin to gain wisdom. No longer do we place worldly things above God. As a result, you begin to produce good fruit for His kingdom. Wisdom is worth more than silver, gold, or other precious gems and comes with a plethora of blessings. What new knowledge or wisdom have you learned today? If you have sought after God with your whole heart today instead of your own desires, then you have gained wisdom.

My song of the say: "Thrive" by Casting Crown
Your song of the day: _____

DAY 5

Yoke to Yearn

"Come to me, all you who are weary and burdened, and I will give you rest. Take my yoke upon you and learn from me, for I am gentle and humble in heart, and you will find rest for your souls. For My yoke is easy, and My load is light.
—Matthew 11:28-30

What Yoke Do You Need to Give to Jesus?

You can see it in their eyes for they tell the story. Dark circles under the eyes always give away the truth regardless of the fake smiles and answers of they are doing fine. When you have a friend whose yoke is heavy and you do not quite know what to say, give them the scriptures in Matthew 11:28-30. It clearly says to come to Jesus. He will give you rest. Take a hold of Jesus's yoke because it is easy and light—no longer live in bondage, weighed down and heavy with fear, despair, or heartache, give it all to Jesus. Allow Him to comfort and guide you into the paths of peace and rest.

Today, we are going to learn how to go from bondage to a yearning desire to learn more about Jesus.

Look up the following words and write their definitions:

Come: _____
Weary: _____
Burdened: _____
Yoke: _____
Gentle: _____
Humble: _____
Rest: _____

Yoke

My biggest yoke was the secret I was hiding from my parents. How much easier life would have been if I had just told them when it had happened. I went through life worried about what others thought of me because I thought the worst of me. Finally, I came to the conclusion that no one was going to think worse thoughts about me than the ones I've already had. And does it really matter if they do? I now know who I am in Christ and that is all that matters.

The Bible in 2 Corinthians 12:10 has new meaning for me: "That is why, for Christ's sake, I delight in weaknesses, in insults, in hardships, in persecutions, in difficulties. For when I am weak, then I am strong."

Read Leviticus 26:13. Do you believe God breaks our yokes? How should we hold our heads?

_____
_____
_____

Read 2 Corinthians 12:7-10. Can a thorn in the flesh be a yoke?

_____
_____
_____

Read Luke 4:18. What have Christians been given? What are we to proclaim when the Spirit of the Lord is upon us?

_____
_____
_____
_____

Read Galatians 5:1. What do we have in Christ? What are we commanded not to let ourselves be burdened with again?

_____
_____
_____

Who sets us free? _____
What do we have freedom from? _____

Read Isaiah 9:1-7. What results when our yoke is removed? What yoke do you need to give to Jesus?

_____
_____
_____
_____

Yearn

The Internet's definition of *yearn* is "to have an intense feeling of longing for something, typically something that one has lost or been separated from."

Long, yearn, hanker, pine, hunger, and *thirst* means "to have a strong desire for something," according to *Merriam-Webster. Long* implies a "wishing with one's whole heart and often a striving to attain."

Read Psalm 84:2. Is this verse true of you? _____

Read Psalm 63. According to Psalm 63, what blessings did David receive when he earnestly sought, thirst, or longed for God?

_____
_____
_____

Learn

Read 2 Timothy 3:16-17. How does the servant of God become equipped for every good work?

_____
_____
_____

Read Deuteronomy 31:9-13. For what reason were the men, women, and children gathered together at the end of every seven years during the Festival of Tabernacles?

_____
_____
_____

Read Proverbs 1:5. A wise man will increase in learning. Those who search for discernment will get _____.

Read Matthew 11:28-29. Who are we to learn from? What do you receive when you learn from Jesus?

_____
_____
_____

This journey of Bible study is like a scavenger hunt created by God—one verse leads to another and so forth. How blessed we truly are when we dig deep into God's Word!

Read Ephesians 4:24-32. Describe your new self.

_____
_____
_____

Read Proverbs 15:33. What comes before wisdom? What comes before honor?

_____
_____
_____

Read Luke 4:16-21. As Jesus read from the scroll, what did He teach in the synagogues in Nazareth?

_____
_____
_____

Read Isaiah 48:17. What does the Lord your God teach you?

_____
_____
_____

What has held you in a yoke of slavery?

_____
_____
_____

Has the thought of being free of that yoke made you yearn to learn more about Jesus? _____

Read Galatians 5:1 and fill in your name in the blank: I, _____ will never again let anyone, including myself, put a yoke of slavery on me.

God never grows tired of hearing our cries or concerns. At times, we can become bogged down by trying to meet the needs of so many people, but our Heavenly Father never grows tired or weary. In fact, He wants us to come to Him with more and more. He wants us to rely on Him for everything. As Adrian Rogers said in his book *What Every Christian Ought to Know*:

"When the child of God
Loves the Word of God
And sees the Son of God
He is changed by the Spirit of God
Into the Image of God
For the Glory of God
Because he has found the truth of God."

People can try to hide it, but eventually it will show if they have a yoke of slavery. No one has to carry that burden. Give it to Jesus for His yoke is easy. He will give you freedom, recovery, and favor. Yearn to learn His word and carry Jesus with you wherever you go instead of that yoke you've carried for too long. Find rest for your soul through Him. Remember Psalm 59:16-17:

> But as for me, I shall sing of Thy strength; Yes, I shall joyfully sing of Thy lovingkindness in the morning, For Thou hast been my stronghold, And a refuge in the day of my distress. O my strength, I will sing praises to Thee; For God is my stronghold, the God who shows me lovingkindness.

My song of the day: "Better Is One Day" by Kutless
Your song of the day: _____

WEEK 2 DISCUSSION

Day 1. When you truly dig into God's word regarding your life patterns or habits, what areas of sin (omission and commission) do you uncover?
_____
_____
_____

Day 2. How can you turn your iniquity to an example in order to have a positive influence on the lives of others?
_____
_____
_____

Day 3. How does God see us through the saving grace of Jesus?
_____
_____
_____

Day 4. How do you take hold of your part of the tree of life?
_____
_____
_____

Day 5. What has held you in a yoke of slavery? Has the thought of being free of that yoke made you yearn to learn about Jesus?
_____
_____
_____

Insights to share:
_____
_____
_____
_____
_____

WEEK 3

On

DAY 1

On Guard

Be of sober spirit, be on the alert. Your adversary, the devil, prowls about like a roaring lion, seeking someone to devour.
—1 Peter 5:8

Which Buttons Does Satan Push to Steer You Away from Jesus Christ?

As an overprotective mother—or *helicopter mom*, as the term goes—I was constantly on guard for things that might hurt my children. My mind could imagine countless ways my children could be harmed. Playing those events in my head over and over again put me in a state of unease, panic, and worry.

This anxiety became worse when my children began to drive and onto young adulthood. One of the hardest days of my life was leaving my daughter at college. I'm not quite sure if it was easier knowing that the campus police was right across the street from her dorm or not. It was frightening to send her out alone in the world. I had to keep reminding myself that she was not alone. God is always with her, and He's better at protecting her than I ever was.

There was no peace to be found when I let my guard down to worry and fear. The realization that worry became wrong overthinking on my part hit home. I needed to reverse it and rely on our deliverer in order to be set free from the worry and fear that creeps in from time to time. I finally learned that fear is not the same thing as being on guard.

Read 2 Peter 3:17-18 and fill in the missing blanks: "You therefore, beloved, knowing this beforehand, be ____ your _____ lest, being carried away by the error of unprincipled men, you fall from your own steadfastness, but grow in the grace and knowledge of our Lord and Savior Jesus Christ. To Him be the glory, both now and to the day of eternity. Amen."

Read Mark 14:38. What are we to do in order not to fall into temptation? _____

Read Luke 4:1-13 when Satan tempts Jesus in the wilderness. List the three temptations Satan tried to lure Jesus with:

Temptation 1: _____
Temptation 2: _____
Temptation 3: _____

The first temptation was to satisfy his physical body by turning stones into bread. The second temptation was material in nature and power by promising to give him all the kingdoms in the world and authority over them. The third temptation was testing His power by tempting Jesus to demonstrate the power He has over the angels to rescue Him if He were to throw Himself off the highest point of the temple. Satan even used scriptures in this temptation.

Jesus was tempted immediately after being baptized in the Jordan River. Remember, temptation is not a sin. It is what you do with the temptation. Are you lured by it or do you stand firm on Christ the Solid Rock and use your spiritual weapons to combat those temptations?

Read Proverbs 4:23 (NIV) and fill in the missing words: "Above all else, _____ _____ _____, for it is the wellspring of life."

Proverbs 4:23 NASB states it this way: "Watch over your heart with all diligence, for from it flow the springs of life." Be diligent, beloved, to watch, guard, and protect your heart from the adversary.

Read James 4:6-7. When we submit to God, we are acting in humble obedience to His will for our lives. Who does God show favor to? _____

Let's "grow in the grace and knowledge of our Lord Jesus Christ" by digging into scripture that will help us to become more obedient.

Write a sentence to yourself based on each of the following scriptures in order to guard your heart:

Adultery (Matt. 5:27-28):
_____
_____

Darkened (Rom. 1:21):
_____
_____

Desire (Rom. 10:1):
_____
_____

Doubt (Mark 11:23):
_____
_____

Evil (Gen. 6:5; Ps. 28:2-3):
_____
_____

Far away (Matt. 15:8):
_____
_____

Fear (Isa. 35:4):
_____
_____

Greed (2 Pet. 2:14):
_____
_____

Hardness (Exod. 4:21; Matt. 19:8; Eph. 4:18):
_____
_____

Hatred (Lev. 19:17):
_____
_____

Lust (Rom. 1:24):
_____
_____

Rebellious (Jer. 5:22-24):
_____
_____

Sorrow or trouble (John 14:1):
_____
_____

Thoughts (Matt. 9:4):
_____
_____

Unrepentant (Rom. 2:5):
_____
_____

Write a sentence to yourself based on each of the following scriptures in order to have a heart like His:

Christ-like (1 John 3:2):
_____
_____

Glad (Acts 2:26):
_____
_____

Good (Luke 6:45):
_____
_____

Hope (Ps. 147:11):
_____
_____

Love (Mark 12:30, 33):
_____
_____

Meditation (Ps. 19:14):
_____
_____

Obedience (Rom. 6:17):
_____
_____

Peace (Jer. 29:11):
_____
_____

Purpose (2 Cor. 9:7):
_____
_____

Renewed (2 Cor. 4:16):
_____
_____

Strong (Phil. 4:13):
_____
_____

Write Colossians 3:12-17. Underline each word that describes which kind of heart you should put on.

Memorize 1 John 2:15-17. Read Psalm 141:3 and fill in the missing words: "Set a _____, O Lord, _____ _____ _____; keep watch over the door of my _____."

Read Psalm 91:11 and fill in the missing words: "For He will give ____ _____ _____ concerning you, to _____ you in all your ways."

Read Psalm 25:20 and fill in the missing words: "_____ my _____ and _____ me; do not let me be _____, I take _____ in _____."

Read Proverbs 13:6 (NIV). What guards the person of integrity?

_____
_____
_____

Read Ephesians 6:18. When should you pray?

_____
_____
_____

Be on guard against Satan's ploys. Remember, he tries to get you to focus on the two bad things instead of focusing on the 98 blessings around you.

What are your trigger points or buttons Satan pushes to steer you away from living an abundant life for Christ?

_____
_____
_____

Read Psalm 27:1. How is the Lord described in this verse? Whom shall you fear?

_____
_____
_____

Read Philippians 4:7. I am so thankful for the promise in this verse. According to Philippians 4:7, what guards your hearts and minds in Christ Jesus?

_____
_____
_____

Ponder that blessed peace provided by our loving God. Once you recognize the trigger points that Satan tries to use to steer you away from living an abundant life for Christ, you can almost see it coming and pray it away. The Lord is the stronghold of your life. He has you in the palms of His hands each and every day. There's nothing to fear, just be on the alert and pray your worries away. Remember

Proverbs 29:6: "By transgression an evil man is ensnared, but the righteous sings and rejoices."

My song of the day: "Whom Shall I Fear?" by Chris Tomlin
Your song of the day: _____

DAY 2

On Christ the Solid Rock I Stand

Trust in the Lord forever, for the Lord, the Lord himself, is the Rock eternal.
—Isaiah 26:4

In What Way Is Jesus Your Rock?

Have you ever felt like running? You get a bad evaluation at work, you get bad news about your health, or things just seem to be out of sorts with your life. Is your tendency to want to run from it? Is your first reaction to run, run to a different job, quit the difficult thing, or crawl in bed for a few days?

Instead of running from problems, I believe God tells us in His word to stand. Stand firm. Stand on Christ the Solid Rock.

Read Ephesians 6:10-20. How can we stand on Christ the solid rock?

_____
_____
_____

What is our struggle against?

_____
_____
_____

How many times is the word stand written in Ephesians 6:10-20? _____

Write each verse below that uses the word *stand*:

Rock

The first mention of the word *rock* was mentioned in Numbers 20:11. It shows the sin of Moses as he struck the rock to bring forth water. The consequence of this sin was the entire Israelite community could not enter into the Promised Land. The verse says, "Because you did not trust in me enough to honor me as holy in the sight of the Israelites, you will not bring this community into the land I give them" (Num. 20:12, NASB).

Moses did not trust the Lord. He did not obey the Lord's command to speak to the rock to allow God to make the water come forth from it. As a result of his sin, his entire community endured forty years in the wilderness and did not enter into the Promised Land. This story is a lesson in always obeying God and give Him the credit for everything. Lean on the Rock, our Lord and our Savior.

The introduction to the book of Numbers in the NASB Bible says this: "While it may be necessary to pass through wilderness experiences, one does not have to live there. For Israel, an eleven-day journey became a forty-year agony." Alternatively, the New American Standard Bible:

> One year for every day spent by the twelve spies in inspecting the land. "Only Joshua and Caleb the two spies who believed God, entered Canaan.
>
> Unbelief brings discipline and hinders God's blessing. Numbers records two generations, two numberings, two journeyings, and two sets of instructions. It illustrates both the kindness and severity of God and teaches that God's people can move forward only as they trust and depend on Him.

Rocks were used for altars, idol worship, protection, shade, inscriptions, executions, foundations, shelters, and tombs. These examples show how rocks were used for both good and bad. We must stand on Christ, who is our solid rock, for protection, our foundation, and shelter. We must worship Him! Stand firm on Christ the solid rock!

Read Mark 15:46 then draw a picture representing this verse.

This picture captures the essence of why we need to stand on Christ the solid rock. Jesus died for us, was placed in a tomb with a large stone placed in front of it, and was raised from the dead. The story doesn't end with placing Jesus in the tomb. Jesus is living in the heavenly realms waiting for our story to be completed so we can join Him. Finish the picture by representing Jesus as risen and alive.

What do the following scriptures say about Christ the Rock?

    Psalm 118:22: _____
    Matthew 21:42: _____
    Romans 9:33: _____
    1 Corinthians 10:4: _____
    1 Peter 2:4: _____

In order to stand on Christ, the solid rock, we must trust Him at all times.

Trust

Read Isaiah 26:4 (NASB) and fill in the missing words: "Trust in the Lord forever, For in God the Lord, we have an _____ _____."

Read the following scriptures about trust and write down your insights for each:

Job 13:15

_____
_____

Psalm 22:4

_____
_____

Psalm 28:7

_____
_____

Psalm 31:14-15

_____
_____

Psalm 131:1-3

_____
_____

Isaiah 43:10

_____
_____

Isaiah 45:9

_____
_____

Matthew 6:33-34

_____
_____

John 6:35-40

_____
_____

Hebrews 2:13

_____
_____

Hebrews 11:1

_____
_____

Read the following scriptures and fill in the missing words:

Deuteronomy 32:3-4: "For I proclaim the name of the _____; ascribe greatness to our _____! The _____! His work is perfect, for all His ways are _____; a God of _____ and without injustice, _____ and _____ is He."

1 Samuel 2:2: "There is no one holy like the Lord, indeed, there is no one besides Thee, nor is there any _____ like our _____."

2 Samuel 22:2-3: "And he said, the Lord is my _____ and my _____ and my _____; My God, my _____ in whom I take refuge; My shield and the horn of my salvation, my _____ and my _____; My _____, Thou dost save me from violence."

Psalm 18:1-3: "I love Thee, O Lord, my _____." The Lord is my _____ and my _____ and my _____, My God, my _____, in whom I take refuge; My _____ and the horn of my _____, my _____. I call upon the _____, who is worthy to be praised, and I am saved from my enemies."

Psalm 18:31-32: "For who is God, but the _____? And who is a _____, except our _____, the God who girds me with _____, and makes my way _____?"

Psalm 27:5: "For in the day of trouble He will conceal me in His tabernacle; in the secret place of His tent He will hide me; He will _____ me _____ on a _____."

Psalm 31:3: "For Thou are my _____ and my fortress; for Thy name's sake Thou wilt lead me and guide me."

Psalm 62:6: "He only is my _____ and my _____, my _____; I shall not be _____."

Psalm 95:1: "O come, let us sing for joy to the Lord; let us shout joyfully to the _____ of our _____."

Isaiah 51:1: "Listen to me, you who pursue righteousness, who seek the Lord; Look to the _____ from which you were hewn, and to the _____ from which you were dug."

After filling in the blanks, what did you discern from the above scriptures?
_____
_____
_____

What do Psalm 118:20-24; Matthew 21:42; and Acts 4:10-12 have in common?
_____
_____
_____

Read Deuteronomy 8:15. What did God bring out of the rock?
_____
_____

Read the following verses and write down what we should always remember:

    Psalm 78:35: _____
    2 Samuel 22:32: _____
    2 Samuel 22:47: _____
    Psalm 18:2: _____
    Psalm 31:2-5: _____

Read Psalm 40:2-3 and fill in the missing words: "He brought me up out of the pit of destruction, out of the miry clay; and He set my feet upon a _____ making my footsteps _____. And He put a new song in my mouth, a song of praise to our God; Many will see and fear, and will trust in the _____."

Read Matthew 16:18 and fill in the missing words: "And I also say to you that you are Peter, and upon this _____ I will build My church; and the gates of Hades shall not overpower it."

Warning: Do not make your face harder than a rock by refusing to repent of your sins (Jer. 5:3).

Read Matthew 7:24. How is your house built?
_____

Challenge: Choose at least three of the above verses to memorize to help you stand on Christ the solid rock. Meditate on His word.

    1.
    2.
    3.

In what ways is Jesus your rock? Draw a picture representing Jesus as your rock.
_____
_____
_____

I love the T-shirt slogan that says, "Jesus is my rock, and that's how I roll." Make Jesus your rock each and every day. Trust Him in all areas of your life. Meditate on His word and stand strong on Christ the solid rock. All other ground is sinking sand.

Stand firm, Beloved! Remember Psalm 95:1: "O Come, let us sing for joy to the Lord; Let us shout joyfully to the rock of our salvation."

My song of the day: "In Christ Alone—Solid Rock" by Travis Cottrell
Your song of the day: _____

DAY 3

On the Lookout

But from there you will seek the Lord your God, and you will find Him if you search for Him with all your heart and all your soul.
—Deuteronomy 4:29

How Often Do We Go through Life and Miss Out on All the Beautiful Things God Wants to Reveal to Us?

Be on the lookout for God! You will surely find Him if you look for Him. Once I began looking for God's love messages, I began seeing more and more of them.

The pivotal moment for me was when I reached my lowest. When you reach your lowest, the only thing left to do is look up. Please do not wait until you reach your lowest before looking up. Start looking up today. God teaches all of us what we need when we need it. His timing is perfect, and for me when I reached my lowest is when I truly became an obedient servant of our Lord Jesus Christ. This journey called our Christian walk does not just happen overnight; it is a process. Every day we get one step closer down the aisle to our Jesus. Savor the journey.

It is difficult to put into words a wonderful God moment. You have to be there to truly experience the awe and wonder of God's presence. On a routine jog up the road, my special God moment happened.

First, here is a little background information to set the stage for you. During my early forties, I was faced with the biggest transition to date. Both my children went away to college, leaving me with an empty nest. My husband and I love each other dearly, but things were changing that I just was not quite ready for. I had completely delved into the role as a wife and mother, which became my identity above all else. I was suddenly lost and confused about who I was.

Additionally, the thoughts of the dear friends who had come into my life and were no longer there were flashing through my mind. Fears and past experiences were welling up to the surface with all of the tears that were flowing out of me. I felt as if I had cried an ocean over a period of just a few short months. On my usual jog, I listened to contemporary Christian music and cried big, ugly, inconsolable, crocodile tears. I felt as if everything near and dear to me was leaving.

I reached the top of the hill, exhausted with sweat pouring from my forehead, tears streaming down my cheeks, and I stretched my hands up toward heaven. I actually said aloud, "God, I give it all to you. Heal my brokenness." At that moment, I noticed a solitary leaf gently floating down from a tree to the ground. The leaf itself was in the shape of a heart with two little hearts at the top that were probably made by a bug needing a snack one day. On the back of the leaf covering the small heart-shaped holes was a spider web.

It was my special message that God loves me—He hears my cries, and He will mend my broken heart as what Psalm 34:18 says: "The Lord is near to the brokenhearted and saves those who are crushed in spirit." It was here that I fell completely head over heels in love with my God!

Since then, I began looking for hearts everywhere. It was my constant reminder that God was there. He's always there. I found them in many other leaves, in clouds, and in flower bushes. On a hike in Tennessee, I even found a heart-shaped rock.

Exactly one year from the day of receiving my first heart leaf, God sent me another one. I was sitting on the dock trying to memorize the first chapter of 1 Thessalonians when I noticed a little ripple in the water. There in the lake was a single leaf with nothing else around it but the beautiful water. When it got close enough to the dock, I reached down to pick it up. It was a green leaf with a small heart-shaped hole in the middle of it. It was brighter and more cheerful looking than the yellow-and-brown leaf from the previous year. It was my love message from God that he was working on the inside to restore my broken heart and heal my hurts.

Whenever I see hearts, I simply say, "I love you too, God." Beth Moore suggested adding the *too* to that expression in the *Children of the Day* Bible study. Adding that little word to the phrase I love you has made a huge impact in my life. It reminds me that God loves me. He loved me first. I love Him too! "We love because He first loved us" (1 John 4:19), His Word says.

Describe a special God moment that you have experienced. If you cannot think of one, then be on the lookout for a special God moment coming your way.

Read Proverbs 8:17. God loves us and as long as we seek after Him we will find Him. What is the definition of *seek*? _____

_____

How often do we go through life in a daze or hurried and miss out on all the beautiful things God wants to reveal to us?

_____
_____

Read Hebrews 10:22 and fill in the blanks: "Let us _____ _____ to _____ with a _____ _____ and with the full assurance that _____ brings, having our _____ sprinkled to _____ us from a guilty _____ and having our bodies _____ with pure _____."

Read James 4:8. What are we directed to do? What does God do as a result of drawing near to Him?

_____
_____
_____

Constantly be on the lookout for God's marvelous gifts and blessings. Here are three things to be on the lookout for:

1. Be on the lookout for God's gifts
2. Be on the lookout for areas of temptation
3. Be on the lookout for lost souls

There are too many to count, but make a list of just a few of God's gifts to you.

Even Jesus looked to God for His gifts when he asked a blessing on the loaves and fish in Matthew 14:19-21, which states,

> And ordering the multitudes to recline on the grass, He took the five loaves and two fish, and looking up toward Heaven, He blessed the food, and breaking the loaves He gave them to the disciples, and the disciples gave to the multitudes, and they all ate, and were satisfied, and they picked up what was left over of the broken pieces, twelve full baskets. And there were about five thousand men who ate, aside from women and children.

The second thing to be on the lookout for are areas of temptation in your own life. Galatians 6:1 states, "Brethren, even if a man is caught in any trespass, you who are spiritual, restore such a one in a spirit of gentleness, each one looking to yourself, lest you too be tempted." Underline the phrase *looking to yourself*. I want to focus on the love chapter in 1 Corinthians for this section. We must examine ourselves for all areas of temptation, but today let us look closely within to see if we are showing love to our family and friends.

Read 1 Corinthians 13. Based on this scripture, what is love?
_____
_____
_____

Based on this scripture, in what areas do you need to work on?
_____
_____
_____

Read 1 Peter 4:8. What are we to do? How are we to love others? What does love cover?
_____
_____
_____

Last, be on the lookout for lost souls. Make a list of family and friends who are lost. Then, pray for them daily as well as those people you haven't met yet who still do not know the saving grace of Jesus.

Read Psalm 51:12-13. Does the joy of your salvation show to others you come in contact with? _____

Read 2 Peter 3:8-18. List the things to look forward to mentioned in 2 Peter 3:8-18:
_____
_____
_____

How do we want to be found by Jesus?
_____
_____
_____

Read 1 Corinthians 2:9. Are you as excited as I am to see the things God has prepared for those who love him?
_____

JUST DIRT ON THE DRESS

_____
_____

Read Jeremiah 29:11-13. What kind of emoji's come to mind after reading these verses? Draw them here.

Hide these truths in your heart:

1. God loves you!
2. Jesus died to redeem you and make you right with God.
3. Jesus is coming again to take you to your heavenly home.

In conclusion,

> be on the lookout for God's love letters and messages,
> be on the lookout for areas of temptation in your life, and
> be on the lookout for lost souls that you can witness to.

Psalm 51:12 says, "Give me a willing spirit to do what's right knowing that it is the only way to have pure joy." Dear Lord, I pray that I always have a willing spirit to do what's right. Help me not to miss your love messages as I seek your presence. Guide me into the paths of righteousness so I might not sin against you. Lead me to the lost and provide the words to say to lead them to you, O Lord! Keep in mind Psalm 42:8: "The Lord will command His lovingkindness in the daytime; and His song will be with me in the night, a prayer to the God of my life."

My song of the day: "Overwhelmed" by Big Daddy Weave
Your song of the day: _____

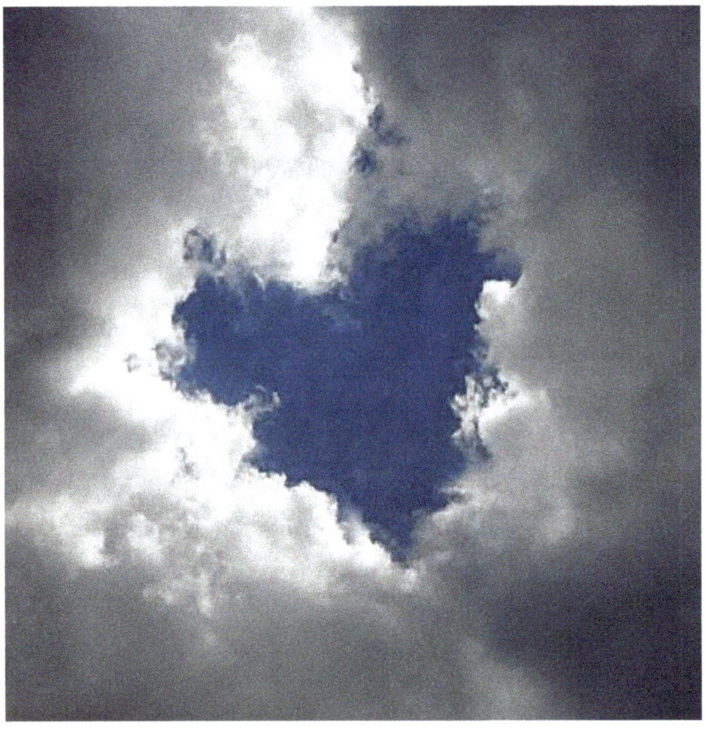

DAY 4

On Cloud Nine

Behold, He is coming with the clouds, and every eye will see Him, even those who pierced Him; and all the tribes of the earth will mourn over Him. Even so. Amen.
—Revelation 1:7

What Would Your "On Cloud Nine" Moment Look Like?

One of my favorite things to do at the lake is lay on my hot-pink float on a beautiful day gazing at the clouds. Trying to form pictures out of them is still a joy. Perhaps I'm still a kid at heart. Anticipating what God might show me that day makes it even more joyful. No one knows the day our Lord Jesus will make His return. What a glorious day it will be to behold our Lord Jesus coming with the clouds!

Isn't it amazing how God can turn a hard day or season in life into a beautiful blessing? A hard day in my life resulted in the richest blessing from God. In April of my junior year in high school, everyone going to the junior-senior prom was able to check out of school early in order to get dressed and ready for his or her special prom night.

Obviously, those not attending the prom were the few students in class that afternoon, and I was one of them. Of course, the young man that I wanted to ask me asked someone else. No one asked me. No one. I'm very old-fashioned, so I stayed home that night because if a guy didn't ask me, I didn't go. I felt unlovable, ugly, and different; but this hard day made me appreciate the cloud nine moment that was just ahead.

The vision of me on my knees in front of our family room plaid couch is as vivid to me today as it was that day back in April of 1986 when I poured my heart out to God. I prayed like I had never prayed before with confessions flowing out and pleadings for Him to send someone who would love me. Some prayers take a long time to be answered; however, this prayer did not.

By July, I learned that a gentleman whom I had known for several years as my brother's friend was interested in asking me out on a date. He hesitated due to our age difference. Four years is not that big of a gap when you're twenty-six and thirty; however, sixteen and twenty seems like a bigger deal especially to protective parents. I will forever be grateful that my parents agreed that we could date.

Even though Jera had graduated from high school four years prior, he willingly took me to my senior prom. From the day of that first phone call asking me out to the present, I remain on cloud nine. Each day, I wake up with my answered prayer—God's chosen companion for me while on this earth, my example of unconditional love, and my reason for being on cloud nine.

When a young lady falls in love, you often hear that she's on cloud nine. What does that mean?

_____
_____

Being on *cloud nine*, according to Urbandictionary.com, is a "feeling of extreme happiness or euphoria, a feeling like you're floating on air." What would your "on cloud nine" moment look like?

_____
_____
_____
_____

Perhaps your "on cloud nine" moment would be walking hand in hand with Jesus with an overwhelming sense of peace and serenity while being surrounded by beauty.

Do you think it's possible to sustain an on cloud nine attitude about life and relationships? If so, how?

_____
_____
_____

Attitude is everything. Allow God's joy and peace that surpasses all understanding to envelope you each and every day. God can cover even the darkest of days and tumultuous storms with tremendous peace.

What reference is made about a cloud in the following verses?

JUST DIRT ON THE DRESS

Genesis 9:13: _____
Exodus 13:21: _____
Exodus 20:21: _____
Exodus 24:15: _____
Exodus 33:10: _____
Matthew 24:30: _____
Luke 21:27: _____
Acts 1:9: _____

Now, write the verse which corresponds with the following references to clouds from the previous verses:

A cloud received Him out of their sight _____
A cloud would speak to Moses (the Lord) _____
Moses approached the thick cloud _____
A pillar of cloud by day _____
A cloud covered the mountain _____
In a cloud with power and great glory _____
The Son of man coming on the clouds _____

I don't think it's a coincidence that the first mention of *clouds* in the Bible is for a wonderfully beautiful reason. In Genesis 9:13, it states that God placed "my bow in the clouds," referring to the rainbow after the flood. The rainbow in the cloud is a symbol of God's covenant to never destroy all mankind again with a flood. It is a beautiful reminder that thrills my soul every time I see one.

When my family and I were on a Disney cruise exploring its private island, I'm positive I saw a cloud that looked like Mickey Mouse ears. Fast forward years later, we saw a cloud in the shape of a baby with a perfect little foot as I looked out on our way home from visiting with our baby grandson born just days prior. These images, however, fail in comparison to the majestic splendor of our Lord Jesus in the clouds coming for us at His great return. We most certainly will be amazed!

J. Stephen Lang describes the many times we read *cloud* in the Bible: In describing Jesus's ascension into heaven, Acts says that "he was taken up before their very eyes, and a cloud hid him from their sight" (Acts 1:9). This is one of many passages in the Bible in which clouds symbolize the divine presence. When Moses ascended Mt. Sinai to meet with God, a cloud covered the mountain (Exod. 24:15), and many other times in the Moses saga a pillar of cloud indicates God's presence. At Solomon's dedication of the Lord's temple in Jerusalem, a cloud filled the temple (1 Kings 8:10). At Jesus's transfiguration, when he was speaking with the long-dead Moses and Elijah, a "bright cloud" enveloped the three men (Matt. 17:5). Jesus prophesied that when he again returned to earth on the Day of Judgment, he would appear "on the clouds of the sky" (Matt. 24:30). The letter to the Hebrews uses the interesting phrase "a cloud of witnesses," referring to the departed saints who are now in the presence of God (Heb. 12:1).

Read *Solomon's temple dedication to the Lord* in 1 Kings 8:10-12. Describe the cloud in the Temple built by Solomon for the Lord and what it represents.

_____
_____

Read the *Voice in the cloud* in Matthew 17:5. What did the voice out of the cloud say?

_____
_____

Read Jesus's *Ascension* in Acts 1:9-11. Why were the men of Galilee gazing intently into the sky in these verses?

_____
_____

Read *God's divine presence* in Exodus 24:15 again. How long did Moses wait before the Lord appeared to him in the midst of the cloud? How long do you wait in the presence of the Lord?

_____
_____

Is it hard for you the Be Still and Know that He is God? Why?

_____
_____

Read the *cloud of witnesses* in Hebrews 12:1. What are a cloud of witnesses?

_____
_____

Read 1 Thessalonians 4:16-17. Where will the dead in Christ meet Jesus?

_____
_____

Our Lord Jesus dances over us as cumulus clouds float into familiar shapes. Your love for me, Jesus, puts me on cloud nine. Do as Psalm 147:7-8 says:

> Sing to the Lord with thanksgiving; Sing praises to our God on the lyre, Who covers the heavens with clouds, Who provides rain for the earth, Who makes grass to grow on the mountains.

My song of the day: "Amazed" by Phillips, Craig & Dean
Your song of the day: _____

DAY 5

Onward Christian Soldier

*For God has not given us a spirit of timidity, but of **power** and **love** and **discipline**. (emphasis mine)*
—2 Timothy 1:7

What Ammunition Are You Taking with You as You Go Out into the World?

March onward, Christian soldier! Do not let the enemy scare you! He's got nothing on our God! Call out to God! Whenever you need help, call out to Him! He did not give us a spirit of timidity. He gave us the opposite which is a spirit of strength and courage.

Read Psalm 144:1-2. What words are used to describe God in these verses of scripture?

_____
_____

Do you ever just ponder why things happen? There must be a reason for bizarre or out-of-the-ordinary things to happen. Perhaps, it is to teach you a lesson, overcome fears, or just steer you in the right direction. Some lessons are easier to learn than others, and some lessons come at a great price. For example, accidental shootings occur mainly for the reason of fear. God does not want us to live in fear. He wants us to have a spirit of courage.

Spirit of Courage

Write the insights you gain from the following verses:

Psalm 27:5
_____
_____

Psalm 33:16-22
_____
_____

Joshua 1:9
_____
_____

What does it mean to be strong?
_____
_____

What does it mean to be courageous?
_____
_____

Don't be timid, my friend! God did not give us a spirit of timidity! As what the Bible says, "For God has not given us a spirit of timidity, but of power and love and discipline" (2 Tim. 1:7).

What kind of spirit did God give us?
_____
_____

Power

I love the song "There Is Power in the Blood." It gives me strength to sing, "There is power, power, wonder working power in the blood of the lamb!" Get that tune stuck in your head when you are feeling weak.

Have you noticed the shirts that ask the question, *What's your superpower?* How would you answer that question? God is the Almighty Power—the Alpha and the Omega.

What if we realized that what we are equipped with is mightier than anything we will ever face?

Ephesians 3:20 says "Now to Him who is able to do immeasurably more than we ask or imagine, according to His power that is at work within us." What if we truly believed we could not fail?

Read Ephesians 3:16-20 prayerfully for your friends, family, and yourself.

Are the concepts of God being with you always and that His grace is sufficient for you elusive?

_____

_____

_____

Read Psalm 108:13. What will we gain with God?

_____

_____

The mighty power that created all things in just six days, the strength that calmed a deadly storm, and the power that raised Jesus from the dead is already at work in you. "Guard, through the Holy Spirit who dwells in us, the treasure which has been entrusted to you," the Bible in 2 Timothy 1:14 says. Walk in the power of God; fight with the one in you! Our Lord is the Conqueror! Read what the NASB introduction of the book of Joshua says:

> Victory comes through faith in God and obedience to His word, rather than through military might or numerical superiority." Joshua's original name is Hoshea meaning "Salvation." "Joshua, born a slave in Egypt, becomes a conqueror in Canaan. He serves as personal attendant to Moses, as one of the twelve spies (of whom only he and Caleb believed God), and as Moses' successor. His outstanding qualities are obedient faith, courage, and dedication to God and His Word.

Draw a picture of yourself fully armored with God. Make sure to include the following from Ephesians 6:11-17:

- Helmet of Salvation
- Belt of truth

- Breastplate of Righteousness
- Sword of the Spirit which is the Word of God
- Feet with the Gospel of Peace
- Shield of Faith

Love

God desires to be at the center of your heart daily. Here are seven healthy heart habits to keep in mind:

1. *Love God.* How should you love God? Read Matthew 22:37 and fill in the missing words: "And He said to him, You shall love the Lord Your God With ____ _____ _____, and with ____ _____ _____, and with ____ _____ _____."

2. *Let the love of God circulate throughout your entire being.* Read Mark 12:30 and fill in the missing words: "And You shall love the Lord Your God with ____ _____ _____, and with ____ _____ _____, and with _____ _____ _____, and with _____ _____ _____." Alternatively, Read 2 Thessalonians 3:5 and also fill in the missing words: "And may the Lord direct your _____ into the _____ of _____ and into the _____ of _____."

3. *Be devoted.* Read Colossians 4:2. What should you devote yourselves to?
   _____
   _____
   _____

   Read Romans 12:10-13 and fill in the missing words: "Be devoted ____ ____ _____ _____ _____ _____, give preference to one another in honor; not lagging behind in diligence, fervent in spirit, _____ the Lord; _____ in hope, _____ in tribulation, _____ to _____."

4. *Serve God.* Read 1 Chronicles 28:9. How was Solomon charged to serve God? _____

   Read Psalm 100:2 and fill in the missing words: "_____ the Lord with _____; Come before Him with _____."

5. *Walk in Him.* Read Colossians 2:6 and fill in the missing words: "As you therefore have received Christ Jesus the Lord, so _____ ___ _____."

   Read Micah 6:8; 2 Corinthians 5:7; Galatians 5:16; Ephesians 4:1-3; and Ephesians 5:8. In what ways should we walk in Him?
   _____

6. *Trust God.* Read Proverbs 3:5. What does it mean to you to trust in the Lord with all your heart?

7. *Do God's Will. Read and write Psalm 40:8:*

"It's the little things in life that touch our hearts the most," a popular saying goes. We do not earn our salvation—it is a free gift from our awesome God. What are the little things you do for God each day to express your love for Him? The greatest thing you can give Him is your heart. Say "Here's my heart, Lord." Love Him! Let the love of God circulate throughout your entire being! Be devoted to Him! Serve Him! Walk in Him! Trust Him! Do God's Will! Praise Him! Thank Him! Seek Him!

Discipline

It seems really basic, but follow the Ten Commandments as proclaimed to us in Exodus 20:2-17 and Deuteronomy 5:6-21 to stay on the straight and narrow path.

Ten Commandments

1. You shall have no other Gods before Me.
2. You shall not make for yourself an idol.
3. You shall not worship them or serve them,
4. You shall not take the name of the Lord your God in vain.
5. Honor your father and your mother.
6. You shall not murder.
7. You shall not commit adultery.
8. You shall not steal.

9. You shall not bear false witness against your neighbor.
10. You shall not covet.

Write a word or phrase to describe how you can have discipline in your Christian walk:

Proverbs 3:5-6: _____
Philippians 4:8: _____
James 4:17: _____
Ephesians 6:10: _____
Romans 8:35-39: _____
Psalm 27:14: _____
Matthew 26:41: _____
2 Peter 3:8-11: _____

We have victory in Jesus! The battle is real, but God is all powerful. He gives us the victory as long as we use His weapons and His spirit within us. "Let your faith in God be bigger than your fears," as a t-shirt slogan says.

Prepare for battle. It's a spiritual battle we face each and every day. Box Satan away! Keep your Bible open twenty-four seven. Keep your Bible open and read daily from His word each and every day to get your armor, ammunition, and awesome power from God!

What ammunition are you taking with you as you go out into the world?
_____

Fight with the following:

- Humility
- Gentleness
- Patience
- Forbearance

Fight on your knees in prayer.

Read Psalm 45:3 and fill in the missing words: "_____ your _____ on your side, you _____ one; _____ yourself with _____ and _____."

As we close the lesson for today, I would like to look at 1 Corinthians 15:54-57. Keep in mind that we have the victory! Never forget that. When times get tough, we have the victory! When things don't seem fair, we have the victory! Jesus gives us the victory over death and sin. God did not make us timid. He gave us a spirit of power, love, and discipline. Use His spirit within you to conquer whatever is standing in your way of fulfilling your calling. "Guard, through the Holy Spirit who dwells in us, the treasure which has been entrusted to you," 2 Timothy 1:14 says. Remember what Psalm 81:1 says: "Sing for joy to God our strength."

Alexander the coppersmith did me much harm; the Lord will repay him according to his deeds. Be on guard against him yourself, for he vigorously opposed our teaching. At my first defense no one supported me, but all deserted me; may it not be counted against them. But the Lord stood with me, and strengthened me, in order that through me the proclamation might be fully accomplished, and that all the Gentiles might hear; and I was delivered out of the lion's mouth. The Lord will deliver me from every evil deed, and will bring me safely to His heavenly kingdom; to Him be the glory forever and ever, Amen. (2 Tim. 4:14-18)

My song of the day: "Courageous" by Casting Crown
Your song of the day: _____

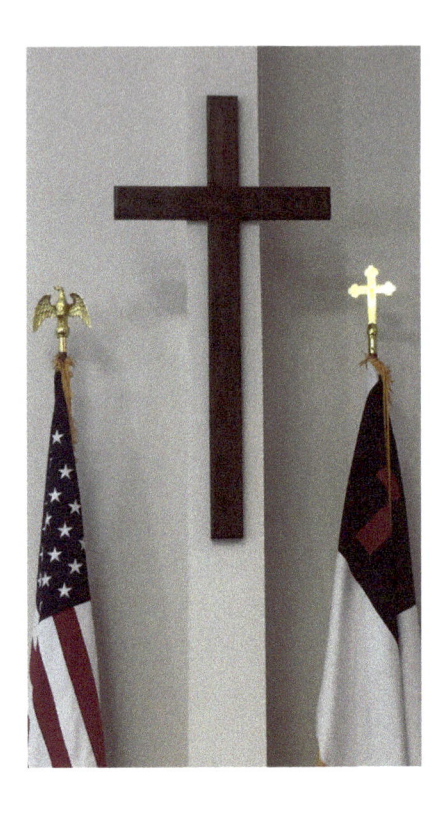

WEEK 3 DISCUSSION

Day 1. What are your trigger points or buttons Satan pushes to steer you away from living an abundant life for Christ?
___

Day 2. In what ways is Jesus your Rock?
___

Day 3. How often do we go through life in a daze or hurried and miss out on all the beautiful things God wants to reveal to us?
___

Day 4. What would your "on cloud nine" moment look like?
___

Day 5. What ammunition are you taking with you as you go out into the world?
___

Insights to share:
___

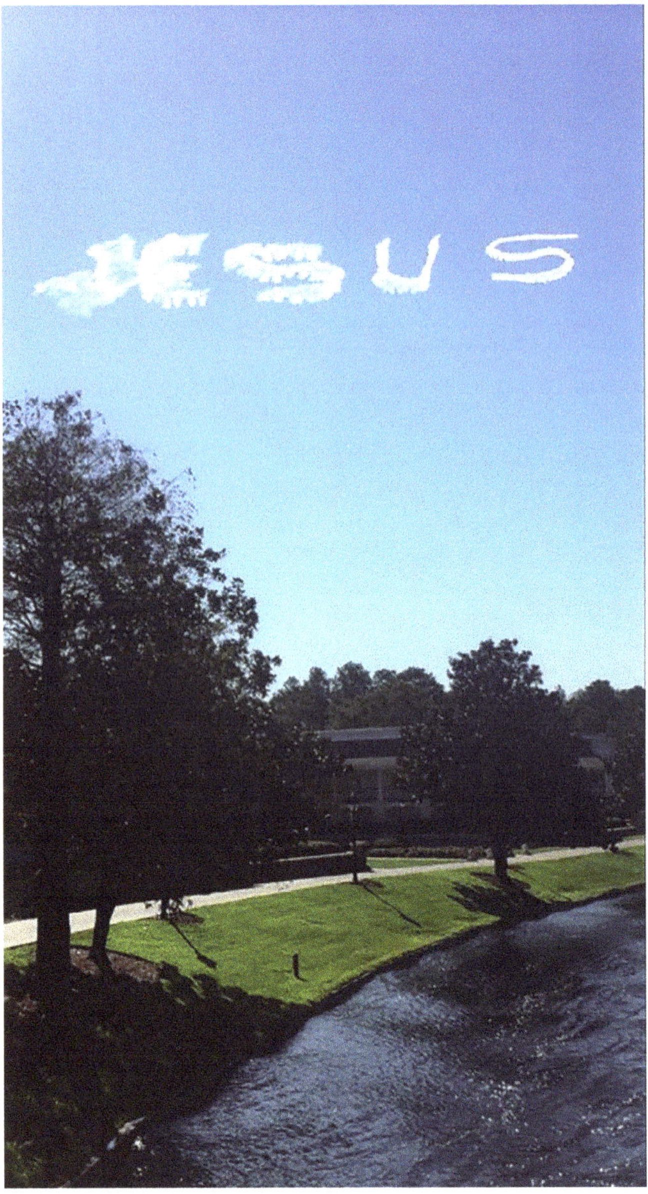
JESUS

WEEK 4

The

DAY 1

The Jesus Is Thy Lord

But whenever a man turns to the Lord, the veil is taken away. Now the Lord is the Spirit; and where the Spirit of the Lord is, there is liberty. But we all, with unveiled face beholding as in a mirror the glory of the Lord, are being transformed into the same image from glory to glory, just as from the Lord, the Spirit.
—2 Corinthians 3:16-18

What Do You See When You Take Off Your Veil?

The time had come in our marriage ceremony for my husband to gently remove the blushing veil away from my face so he could kiss his bride. His eyes stayed on my eyes without a care in the world of what the veil looked like from behind. He bent down from his six-foot-four-inch frame to my five-foot-four-inch self. The kiss was long enough to seal the deal but not too long in front of a crowd of over two hundred onlookers. It was glorious!

I suppose veils are becoming old-fashioned. Neither my daughter nor daughter-in-law wore one on their special wedding day. In an article titled "A History of Wedding Veils" from *Wedding Ideas Magazine* tells us that in ancient times,

> the Greeks used it as a way of protecting the bride from evil spirits, while in Medieval times it was worn as a symbol of purity and chastity. Today it's still seen as quite a formal wedding accessory but thanks to the royal wedding, one that is coming back into fashion.

We see the term *veil* used in several different ways in the Bible pointed out in *The Baker Compact Bible Dictionary*:

In the harsh desert of the Middle East, a veil is useful protection from the sun and windblown sand. While Hebrew women tend to appear without veils. Dressing in veils in public may have been considered appropriate for women of certain status, so that forced removal becomes an act of shaming. However, in the Bible, veils also serve as more than protection from the elements. Rebekah puts on a veil in deference before encountering her future husband, Isaac. Tamar veiled herself in order to deceive Judah, her father-in-law, into sleeping with her. And judgment is said to await the women who make veils of various lengths for their heads in order to ensnare people.

The Veil

Here are some other examples of how the veil was depicted in scripture:

Read Exodus 26:31-35. Describe the inner veil.

_____
_____
_____

Read Exodus 26:36-37. Describe the outer veil.

_____
_____
_____

Read Exodus 30:6 and 40:26. What is in front of the veil that is near the ark of the testimony?

_____

Read Exodus 34:33-35. What could the sons of Israel see through the veil that Moses wore after speaking with God in the temple?

_____

Read Exodus 40:3. What did the Lord instruct Moses to do?

_____

Read Exodus 40:21. What shielded the Ark of the Covenant?

_____

Read Leviticus 4:17. What did the priest do in front of the veil during the sin offering?

_____

Read Numbers 4:5-15. What were Aaron and his sons instructed to do when they were ready to move camp?

_____
_____
_____

Read Numbers 18:7. Who was given charge of being priests? What happens to anyone else who comes near the sanctuary?

_____
_____
_____

Read Matthew 27:50-66. Explain what happened to the veil.

_____
_____
_____

Read Hebrews 6:19-20. What entered the sanctuary behind the veil for all Christians because of our high priest and forerunner, Jesus? _____

What blessed hope we have because of what Jesus did for us! Praise Him!

Read Hebrews 10:19-25. What does the veil (or curtain) represent?

_____
_____
_____

Describe how you feel after reading Hebrews 10:17 "Then he adds: Their sins and lawless acts I will remember no more":

_____
_____

Make the following scripture your prayer: "Let the words of my mouth and the meditation of my heart be acceptable in Thy sight, O Lord, my Rock and my Redeemer" (Ps. 19:14).

I am not always pleased with what comes out of my mouth. Perhaps part of the reason I stay too quiet is for this fact. I do not want to say something that I will later regret. There are times, however, that I have regretted not saying what I feel God placed on my heart to say and did not for fear of how it would be perceived.

Words

Words have lasting power. I know this because even though my grandmother has been in the arms of Jesus for over sixteen years, her tender and precious compliments still make their way to my thoughts from time to time.

As illustrated in Max Lucado's children's book *You Are Special*, we can use our words to create dots or stars on our friends, families, and acquaintances. You put dots on people when you say things that are not uplifting to that person. We ultimately have the choice to determine how those things affect us. We can let those replay in our mind and affect our heart or we can dust off the unpleasant words and go on with our life lighter and freer. The opposite is true as well. Many people are great encouragers and lift others up. They are positive and complimentary. Just their presence fills you with joy. The stars they put on you have lasting power. Always choose to replay the positives instead of the negatives.

God's Word is everlasting. His Word never fades, never changes, and is always pertinent to every generation throughout all time.

What do the following scriptures say about God's Word?

Numbers 23:19: _____
1 Samuel 3:1: _____
Hebrews 4:12: _____

Vows

As a Christian walk begins with words of confession, marriage ceremonies contain vows. Many of us have made the public confession of faith: "I believe that Jesus is the Christ, the Son of the living God." When you make that statement, you are essentially saying that your life will be a testimony declaring it to be true—your walk and talk will match.

What do the following scriptures say about your words or vows?

Numbers 30:2: _____
_____

Deuteronomy 23:23: _____
_____

Ecclesiastes 5:4-7: _____
_____

Matthew 5:33-37: _____
_____

Acts 18:18-22: _____
_____

Read Mark 14:29-31; 66-72. What was Peter's vow to Jesus? Explain what actually happened in these verses.
_____
_____
_____

Are we going to stand on Christ the solid rock and *not* deny Him? We certainly hope so with just as much conviction as Peter felt at that time.

Meditation

What do you meditate on? What do you spend the majority of the day thinking about?

Read Joshua 1:8. What should you mediate on? How often should you meditate on God's Word?
_____
_____

Recite Psalm 19:14 as a prayer.
What do the following scriptures teach you about meditation?

     Psalm 1:2:_____
     Psalm 4:4: _____

Psalm 16:7-8: _____
Psalm 42:1-2: _____
Psalm 42:7-8: _____
Psalm 48:9: _____
Psalm 63:6: _____
Psalm 77:10-14: _____
Psalm 143:5: _____
Luke 5:16: _____
Hebrews 3:1: _____
1 John 2:24-25: _____
Revelation 1:3: _____

Redeemer

Fill in the missing words from Psalm 51:1-9:

Be gracious to me, O God, according to Thy lovingkindness; According to _____ greatness of _____ compassion blot out my transgressions. Wash me thoroughly from my iniquity, and cleanse me from my sin. For I know my transgressions, and my sin is ever before me. Against ____, _____ only, I have sinned, and done what is evil in ___ sight, so that _____ art justified when _____ dost speak, and blameless when _____ dost judge. Behold, I was brought forth in iniquity, and in sin my mother conceived me. Behold, _____ dost desire truth in _____ innermost being, and in ___ hidden part _____ wilt make me know wisdom. Purify me with hyssop, and I shall be clean; wash me, and I shall be whiter than snow. Make me to hear joy and gladness, Let _____ bones which _____ hast broken rejoice. Hide ___ face from my sins, and blot out all my iniquities.

Read John 1:34 (NIV) and fill in the missing words: "And I have seen, and I testify that this is _____ _____ _____."

Make Jesus your Lord, not your cell phone, social media, friends, or family. When Jesus is thy Lord, then you shall be free.

Read Matthew 6:33-34. What promises are we given when we seek first the kingdom of God?

_____

_____

We have been redeemed by the Son of God and sealed by the Spirit, and we will receive our inheritance in Heaven. Praise God!

Jesus Christ treats me just as if I am His chosen beloved, but He is the chosen one. *Christ* is the Greek word for *Christos*, meaning "anointed one" or "chosen one." This is the equivalent of the Hebrew word *Mashiach*, or *Messiah*, according to our-rabbijesus.com. Jesus is the Lord's human name given to Mary by the angel Gabriel (Luke 1:31). *Jesus Christ* means "Jesus the Messiah" or "Jesus the Anointed One."

When we become the Bride of Christ, we are the bride of the anointed one. Jesus is our Lord! By dying on the cross, He gave us salvation and access to pray to our Heavenly Father. Freedom in Christ is ours for the taking. May our words and actions glorify Him. Constantly meditate on the words of God and remember Him with thanksgiving as the Bible teaches us: "But let all who take refuge in Thee be glad, let them ever sing for joy; and mayest Thou shelter them, that those who love Thy name may exult in Thee" (Ps. 5:11).

My song of the day: "Cornerstone" by Hillsong
Your song of the day: _____

DAY 2

The One and Only

For there is one God and one mediator between God and mankind, the man Christ Jesus.

—1 Timothy 2:5

Who Is the One and Only in Your Life?

I have had many wonderful and dear people cross my path over the course of my life. Some still stir up very tender and endearing feelings when I think of them or recall that season of life. When I get a call or even a Facebook like from those certain people, it brightens my whole day. I could have a hundred likes, but just that one special one makes all the difference in the world to me.

Perhaps I put certain people on pedestals without even realizing it. My spouse, children, family members, special friends, and favorite teachers will forever hold a permanent place in my heart for the joy and love they bring to my life. I have to guard against putting them as the one and only, above the true One and Only. Jesus must take first place in our lives each and every day! He alone deserves the pedestal not mere mortals.

What does the phrase *the one and only* mean to you?
_____
_____

One and only can be an adjective or a noun. It means "incomparable"; "unique" according to *Collins Dictionary*. It is the "object of all one's love"—"you are my one and only." Urbandictionary states it as "an eloquent way of expressing your love and devotion for another" such as the following demonstrates:

JUST DIRT ON THE DRESS

1. The only one for me
2. The only one I will ever love
3. Mine (expressing romantic possession)
4. Apple of my eye

Haven't you used or heard these expressions before? "I want to spend the rest of my life with you. You are my one and only." Have you ever stated the following? Jesus, I want to spend the rest of eternity with you; you are my one and only, my savior, my friend, my redeemer, my rock—my everything!

Who is the one and only in your life? _____

Jesus desires to be our one and only. Tell Him so. _____, you are my one and only!

Write Jesus a love letter.

Read Isaiah 9:6 and underline each word or phrase that describes Jesus: "For a child will be born to us, a son will be given to us; and the government will rest on His shoulders; and His name will be called Wonderful Counselor, Mighty God, Everlasting Father, Prince of Peace."

Fill in the blanks:

1. Jesus is our _____!
2. Jesus is our _____!
3. Jesus is our _____!
4. Jesus is our _____!

Wonderful Counselor

Write Psalm 33:11.

_____
_____
_____
_____
_____
_____

How long does the counsel of the Lord stand? _____

Write Psalm 73:24.

_____
_____

After I allow the counsel of the Lord to _____ me, he will _____ me to glory.

How has Jesus been your Wonderful Counselor?

Mighty God

Write Psalm 147:5.

There is _____ limit to His understanding.

Write 1 Corinthians 6:14.

In what ways have you experienced our Mighty God?

JUST DIRT ON THE DRESS

Everlasting Father

Read Genesis 1:1 and fill in the blanks: "In the _____, _____ created the heavens and the earth."

Write 1 Timothy 1:17.

_____
_____
_____
_____
_____
_____

How long shall we give honor and glory to our King? _____

Prince of Peace

Read Ephesians 2:13-18. How do we have access to the Father?
_____
_____
_____

When have you experienced peace during a storm in your life?
_____
_____
_____

One Advocate

Read 1 John 2:1-2 and fill in the missing words: "My dear children, I write this to you so that you will not sin. But if anybody does sin, we have an _____ with the Father—Jesus Christ, the _____ _____. He is the atoning sacrifice for our sins, and not _____ for ours but also for the sins of the _____ _____."

One God

What do the following verses have in common? Write a word or phrase beside each verse to determine the commonality between these verses.

Deuteronomy 4:35
Deuteronomy 4:39
Deuteronomy 6:4
2 Samuel 7:22
1 Kings 8:60
1 Chronicles 17:20
Psalm 86:10
Isaiah 43: 10-11
John 17:3
Ephesians 4:6
1 Timothy 1:17
James 2:19

There is no other God. No, not one!

One Mediator

What is a mediator?

_____
_____
_____

The definition of *mediator* is "a person who attempts to make people involved in a conflict come to an agreement"; "a go-between"; "arbitrator, peacemaker"; and an intercessor.

Write out 1 Timothy 2:5 in the margin. Draw a cross in between Christ and Jesus. The horizontal line represents Jesus interceding for us with God. The vertical line represents all of humanity from one end of the earth to the other for all time. Jesus is the only one who can go to the one and only God to reconcile everyone. Take what Matthew Henry said in *Concise Commentary*:

> There is one Mediator, and that Mediator gave himself a ransom for all. And this appointment has been made for the benefit of the Jews and the Gentiles of every nation; that all who are willing may come in this

way, to the mercy-seat of a pardoning God, to seek reconciliation with him. Sin had made a quarrel between us and God; Jesus Christ is the Mediator who makes peace.

We have an audience of one for which to seek applause from. Do not try to please everyone, just the only one that matters!

Jesus has *the* name above all names. Write as many words or names as you can think of to describe Jesus.

Read Mark 12:29-34. What shall we do according to Mark 12:29-34?

_____
_____
_____

May we exemplify Christ in all that we say, think and do. Collectively, we are the Bride of Christ. All will bow before the One and Only one day. Allow God to give us away to Jesus, the One and Only Savior.

Read Romans 3:30. What will the only one God do for all people, Jews and Gentiles?

_____

Read Ephesians 4:4-6 and underline each reference to one:

There is one body and one Spirit, just as you were called to one hope when you were called; one Lord, one faith, one baptism; one God and Father of All, who is over all and through all and in all.

Write Exodus 20:3 and underline the word no.

My daughter was always asking *why* questions as a little girl: *Why is the sky blue? Why is it dark in space when it is closest to the sun? Why are apples different colors?* She recalls the answer I gave when I couldn't give a good, clear answer to her questions was, because God made it that way, that's how God wanted it, etc. My answer was, God—He's always the right answer! God had the answer for reconciling us back to Him. His answer for our salvation was Jesus. You are my one and only hope for salvation, Jesus! You are my One and Only!

Sing praise to the Lord, you His godly ones, And give thanks to His holy name. (Ps. 30:4)

My song of the day: "Jesus, Only Jesus" by Phillips, Craig & Dean
Your song of the day: _____

DAY 3

The Indescribable Gift

Thanks be to God for His indescribable gift!
—2 Corinthians 9:15

What Was the Best Gift You Ever Received?

My mom is the most selfless person I will ever know! She is always considerate of others, putting everyone before herself and working her fingers to the bone for her family. I praise her because she is the epitome of the Proverbs 31 woman.

On special occasions, I want to give my mom the best gifts. Unfortunately, she is the hardest person to buy for. Everything that I choose to give her just never seems good enough.

What was the best gift you have ever received?
_____
_____

It is a natural thing to want to give gifts to those whom we love. I love having quality time with my loved ones and friends, but I receive great satisfaction and joy when I give gifts to them. It is equally natural to receive gifts from others. Engaged couples go to a variety of stores to complete gift registries because their family and friends want to shower them with wedding gifts.

A lesson I have learned is to accept gifts offered out of friendship or love even if it is not exactly what you want such as a biscuit after you have worked out for an hour at the local gym. If you are offered something from someone, take it. Do not deprive them of the joy of giving

It is a bit embarrassing to admit that some of the feelings I experienced in middle school creep back up in me from time to time while in my forties. My love language is quality time, so when I do not feel like I've had enough time with my family or friends, I become jealous, moody, and sad. Having time with those that I care about makes me happy. This realization caused me to consider whether or not I am showing my love for God with the amount of time I devote to prayer, Bible study, and service for Him.

Read Proverbs 18:16. What does this verse mean?
_____
_____

Read Matthew 2:11. What gifts did Jesus receive from the Magi?
_____
_____

Just like the wise men gave gifts to the baby in the manger, our king on the throne, we too should give gifts to Jesus. He wants our love, our time, and our devotion.

What we have to keep at the forefront of our minds is that Jesus is the best gift anyone could ever want. He is the indescribable gift because He laid down His life for each of us. How, then, can you not accept His wonderful gift? How is it that some people choose to refuse this free gift of salvation? Do you reject the gifts of friends and family on your birthday or Christmas? Why, then, do you reject the greatest gift of all?

Jesus gave us the gift of love. How we show love to Him is by loving others and feeding His lambs. "Loving Jesus is manifested in loving and caring for others (feed my sheep)," John 21:15 says, which David L. Allen so eloquently emphasizes the need for love:

> Love is the circulatory system of the church. If the arteries of love get clogged, the church is in danger of spiritual cardiac arrest. One key evidence of spiritual maturity in our lives is the depth of our love for one another.

God loved us first. We love God and show our love for Him by loving one another.

Let's revisit 1 Corinthians 13:4-8. Draw a heart around the words that represent what love is and draw a line through the items that does not represent love:

> Love is patient, love is kind, and is not jealous; love does not brag and is not arrogant, does not act unbecomingly; it does not seek its own, is not provoked, does not take into account a wrong suffered, does not rejoice in unrighteousness, but rejoices with the truth; bears all things believes all things, hopes all things, endures all things. Love never fails.

Well, let's not play around. Let's come right out of the gate with a hard one: Love is patient. Why is it that some people just have more patience than others? Some have a calming effect on others, while others always seem to be wound up tight all the time. What does patience look like? I've always told my children that patience is waiting without complaining, smiling when you feel like clinching your teeth, and treating others better than you want to be treated yourself.

Love is kind. What are some practical and simple ways you can and do show kindness?

_____

_____

I love the "random acts of kindness" and pay-it-forward movements that have swept the nation. It's a wonderful cycle of expressing love to one another.

Love is not jealous. I love the ease with which my husband has with speaking to strangers. Chitchat comes easy for him. He never meets a stranger because he is soon a friend to all he meets. Wishing that came just as easy for me. I really have to work at not being jealous of the wonderful attributes of my husband.

List the things you may be envious about your spouse or others. Now, give thanks to God for those things as it will change your heart toward them. Remember most feelings of envy and jealousy are rooted by insecurity. Those feelings need to do a complete 180 turnaround, which can be accomplished through prayer. Decide to combat feelings of envy with a prayer of thanksgiving that they have those special gifts. Look for your special gifts and talents that God has blessed you with that make you special and give thanks to God for what makes you unique. Then, get busy using your spiritual gifts for God's glory.

Love is not arrogant or boastful. Have you heard of Proverbs 16:18? "Pride goes before destruction, a haughty spirit before a fall." As soon as you begin to get boastful, things begin to unravel.

"Does not act unbecomingly" is a loaded command. When are you more apt to act unbecomingly? Perhaps you have had a lack of sleep, driving in traffic, or someone hits a nerve. Generally, it's easy to act unbecomingly when you feel as if you do not matter to others. Many times, the way we perceive situations is completely the opposite of reality. Just love others. Always!

Pride is not becoming of a Christian. I'm battling pride by having to admit that I have had low self-esteem. I want everything to be perfect. I want to be perfect. I want your perception of me to be that of a good and decent person; therefore, I try to be perfect in all that I do and say. Here's the reality: I am not perfect, never have been and never will be. What matters is, God's perception of me, and He loves me just the way I am with all my imperfections.

Love does not seek its own. What would this look like? What are some things you can do for others? Seeking out someone to bless is like rocking a newborn baby—it gives you pure joy! You can relate it to picking wildflowers and adorning your house by putting them in a vase on your kitchen table. You have taken something that others ignore or overlook, and you turn it into something beautiful and cherished. Young boys and girls know all about this. They oftentimes will pick flowers for their favorite teachers.

Love never fails. What does that mean?
_____
_____

You always win with love. God is love; therefore, God never fails. Be godly. Choose to be loving when it is easier to be ugly, jealous, judgmental, to retaliate, or otherwise be unbecoming of a Christian.

Would you say your love for others is unconditional or conditional? Does it depend on the person?
_____
_____

How can you make your love for others unconditional like God's love for you?
_____
_____

Read John 13:34-35. What are we commanded to do?
_____
_____

Read Acts 2:38. What gift do you receive when you repent and are baptized in the name of Jesus Christ?
_____
_____

Read Romans 6:23. What is the gift of God?
_____
_____

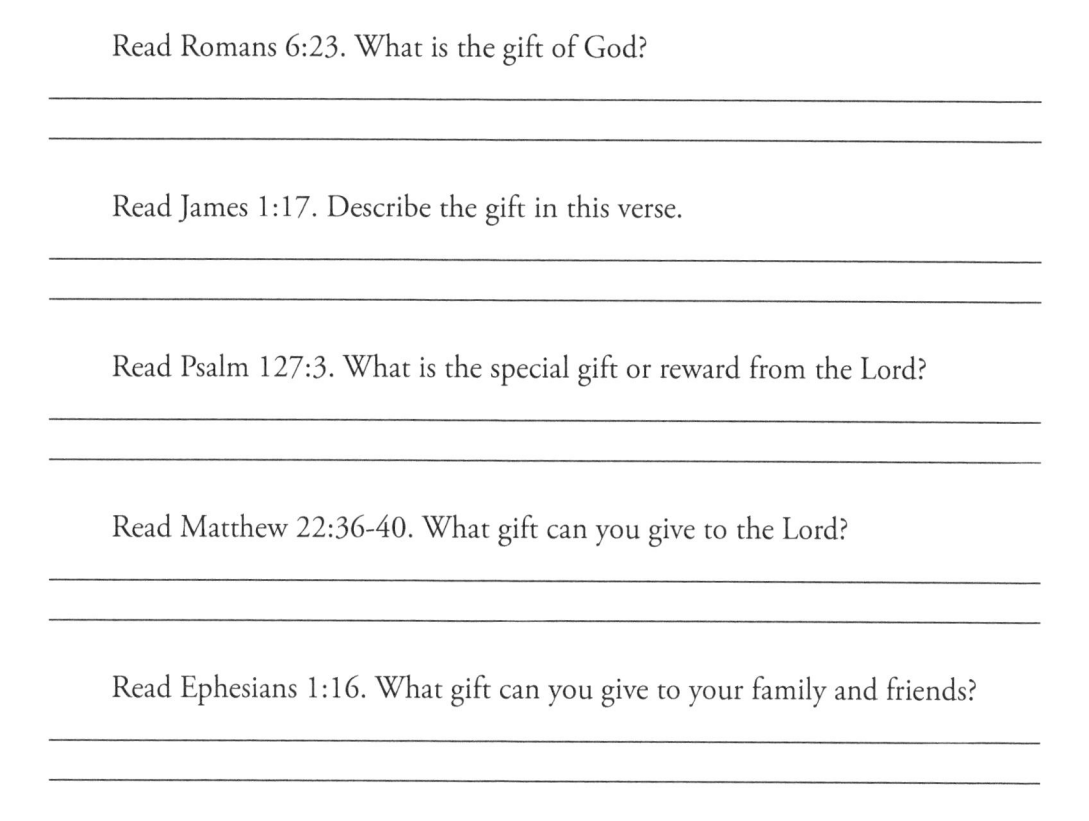

Read James 1:17. Describe the gift in this verse.
_____
_____

Read Psalm 127:3. What is the special gift or reward from the Lord?
_____
_____

Read Matthew 22:36-40. What gift can you give to the Lord?
_____
_____

Read Ephesians 1:16. What gift can you give to your family and friends?
_____
_____

1 John 4:8 states, "He who does not love does not know God for God is love."

We are born of God and God is love; therefore, we are born to love God and others. Have a personal relationship with God. It's more than just church attendance. It's seeking him daily.

As Jeremiah 31:3 says, "I have loved you with an everlasting love; therefore I have drawn you with lovingkindness." Thank you, Lord, for your gift of love!

Dear Jesus,
Dear Jesus, Dear Jesus,
if I could write you a letter
Dear Jesus,
this is what it would say.

Dear Jesus,
I want to say thank you
for being my best friend,
better than my BFF.
My Savior, Redeemer,
Sustainer—
my Everything!

Dear Jesus,
You are my best friend,
showing, guiding, living, dying
for me
all the way to the cross and back!

You gave it all.
You're in my heart
Always near
and oh so dear!

Dear Jesus,
You are my best friend,
showing, guiding, living, dying
for me
all the way to the cross and back!
You saved me,
hope and salvation
you gave me,
full and free!

I can't wait to spend more time with you,
the Great I Am!
Everlasting Life!
Home in Glory!

There's not a better friend
than the one who gave his life
on Calvary.
The greatest gift
sent from Heaven above!

I love you all the more
because you loved me.
Your sacrifice delivers me
from what I deserve.

Dear Jesus,
You are my best friend,
showing, guiding, living, dying

for me
all the way to the cross and back!
My heart smiles when I think of you.
I'll send it up on a balloon.
Love me.
P.S. Come again soon!

After Mary gave birth to Jesus, the shepherds found them in the manger and spread the word about this precious child, the Son of God. "Mary treasured up all these things and pondered them in her heart," it is said in Luke 2:19. When was the last time you stopped to ponder the greatest gift of all?

Write your thank-you note to Jesus for His indescribable gift to you.

_____
_____
_____
_____
_____
_____

Think of Psalm 13:5-6 too: "But I have trusted in Thy lovingkindness; My heart shall rejoice in Thy salvation. I will sing to the Lord, Because He has dealt bountifully with me."

My song of the day: "Someone Worth Dying For" by MIKESCHAIR
Your Song of the Day: _____

DAY 4

The Lord Is My Shepherd

The Lord is my shepherd, I shall not want. He makes me lie down in green pastures; He leads me beside quiet waters. He restores my soul; He guides me in the paths of righteousness for His name's sake. Even though I walk through the valley of the shadow of death, I fear no evil; for Thou art with me; Thy rod and Thy staff, they comfort me. Thou dost prepare a table before me in the presence of my enemies; Thou hast anointed my head with oil; My cup overflows. Surely goodness and lovingkindness will follow me all the days of my life, and I will dwell in the house of the Lord forever.
—Psalm 23

In What Ways Is Your Cup Overflowing with Blessings?

Over the years, I have had many special people cross my path. These dear friends are my "cookie people." They are precious to me and always will be no matter the time or distance apart. One of them is a former teacher. She called me sweetheart, smiled at me, and made me feel special, like I mattered. Even to this day, I have the thank-you notes she wrote me during that year.

Many fond memories flood back to me when I think of her. She was enthusiastic about the subjects she taught, and I was certainly blessed to have her as my teacher for several classes that year. God knew I needed someone as precious as her to love on me during those difficult teenage years. It was as if she was delighted to have me in her class just as much as I was delighted to be in her classes. Oh, how I was motivated to work extra hard because I wanted to please her. I made great strides that year and even began to enjoy reading for pleasure. She has remained in my thoughts and prayers all of these years later. I even remember her birthday and say a prayer for her on her special day each year. She's still a big deal to me.

Have you met someone whom you knew without a doubt you wanted to be your BFF? Have you thought about that person, wanted to be with that person, hang out with them, and just laugh and have a good time with them? Perhaps, there was time or distance that kept you from having such a bond with that special person. Everyone seems too entirely busy these days.

What if that special person was Jesus? What if you decided He was your BFF? Do you want to hang out with Him? Do you want to be with Him above all else? Do you want to talk to him, laugh with Him, tell Him your concerns and problems, cry on His shoulder and no one else? Jesus is all of that and more! There is no time or distance between you. He is always there.

Underline all of the verbs in Psalm 23 at the beginning of the chapter. You will notice that there are past, present, and future tense verbs:

- Verbs to be (is)
- Past tense (has anointed)
- Present tense (makes, leads, restores, guides, walk, fear, art, comfort, prepare, overflows)
- Future tense (will follow, will dwell)

The Lord Is My shepherd

What are the words used to describe the Lord?

_____
_____
_____

Our Lord Jesus Christ is our Shepherd, Leader, Restorer, Guide, Fear Deflector, Comforter, and Preparer/Provider.

What is the meaning of *my cup overflows*?

_____
_____
_____

Fill in the missing words from Psalm 23:

Jesus
Is My _____
Makes Me _____
Leads _____

Restores _____
_____ Me
Art _____
_____ Me
Prepares _____
Anointed _____

I
Shall _____
Walk _____
Fear _____
Have a cup that _____
Have Goodness and _____
_____
Will Live _____

Thank you, Lord, that there's no limit to your love or forgiveness.

Read Isaiah 53:6. What are people compared to in this verse? What is sin that is mentioned in this verse?

_____
_____
_____

Read Acts 20:28. According to this verse, who should be shepherds? In what ways can Christians shepherd the church?

_____
_____
_____

Look back on your life not with regret but with thankfulness at what God has done in your life. How has he seen you through the valleys?

_____
_____
_____

How does He celebrate with you during the joyful times?

_____
_____
_____

I completed my first marathon at the age of forty-seven. Not sure if I'd be able to finish or not, I came prepared with prayer warriors at home, memorized scripture such as the Lord's Prayer and Psalm 23 on my mind, and self-talk pointers on my lips. "One step at a time" was my mantra. I'm not sure what the next step will bring, but I just keep taking the next step. When I put God first in my life, it becomes clearer what the next step should be.

Read John 10:1-18. How is Jesus your shepherd?
_____
_____
_____

With the Lord as *my* Shepherd, I want for nothing. When I'm running a race, I tell myself I shall not want ability, endurance, speed, breath, etc. In daily life, I shall not want for my necessities. He restores my soul when it is damaged from this cruel world. He is with me in the valleys and the joy-filled moments. His promises provide peace and comfort every day of my life.

O sing to the Lord a new song, For He has done wonderful things, His right hand and His holy arm have gained the victory for Him. (Ps. 98:1)

My song of the day: "Overflow" by Newsboys
Your song of the day: _____

DAY 5

The Other Side

For as high as the heavens are above the earth, so great is His lovingkindness toward those who fear Him.
—Psalm 103:11

What Does It Mean to Cross Over to the Other Side?

Floating on my hot-pink float on the lake gives me great joy! At times, the water is as still as a mirrored sheet of glass, and I just stay in one place. At other times, when I open my eyes again, I've discovered that I drifted quite a distance away from the dock, my starting point. It was a gentle current, yet it still caused me to drift unaware.

On special occasions, such as Memorial Day, Fourth of July, and Labor Day, the water is extremely rough and far from the peaceful waters of tranquil days. I enjoy the rough waters on the lake from time to time. What a great ride on the waves! What fun to predict the bobbing up and down that is about to take place as you watch the rolling waves come in! What if we felt the same about our rough waters of life? What if we looked at them as great opportunities to experience God's presence, His peace, and miracles instead of fear, stress, and uncertainty? What if we knew with complete certainty that we will reach the other side? This is our hope in Jesus!

Today, we will learn how to get to the other side: How do we get to the other side of our trials, circumstances, and our sinful self? How will you get to the other side, through fear or faith?

A YouTube video by Jon Jorgenson called "What Are You Afraid Of" explains this eloquently:

> What room does fear have? What room does fear have when I cling to trust? What room does fear have when I lean on hope? What room

does fear have when I search for something more, when I discover what's good, and when I stand in awe? When I run with perseverance, when I walk by faith, and when I rest in comfort? What room does fear have when I sing with praise, when I take hold of inspiration, explore the possibilities and step into freedom? What room does fear have when I discover strength, embrace courage, remember peace, declare truth, choose joy, experience life, and conquer death? What room does fear have when I find perfection in the one place I never thought to look, in weakness, when I'm saved by the most unlikely of heroes. By grace, when I'm invited into a relationship more loving and intimate than I could ever imagine as a child of God. I'll ask you again: what room does fear have when I step out of the darkness, and I bask in the light? When I let the past be the past and the future has no limit. When they can talk all they want but their opinion doesn't matter. And when failure is nothing more and nothing less than the road by which I walk my path to success. I'll ask you one last time: what room does fear have when in His Word, He tells me three hundred and sixty-five times, depending on the translation, do not be afraid. As if I needed to hear that every single day. And as if that's how many times I needed to hear it before I finally believed it. What room does fear have when I make room for love? What are you afraid of?

Read Mark 4:35-41. Write the questions from these scriptures:

_____
_____
_____
_____
_____

What does Jesus say to the storm?

_____
_____

What should we say to ourselves when we feel fear creeping in our thoughts and lives?

_____
_____
_____

Do you ever wish parts of you were made with Velcro so if you didn't like a part of your personality or a certain trial you are going through, you could just take it off and replace it with what you like? When you are amid trials or revisit places of hurt, you can almost hear the rip of your heart such as when you separate the Velcro pieces. The kids leaving for college then marriage ripped a hole in my heart that only God could mend. Still to this day, I miss the time when it was the four of us together; however, look at what I have gained in exchange for the change that was inevitable: more people in my life to love. This is what we strive for as parents. Our goal is to train up our children to be independent and live their own lives.

In contrast, we are children of God, yet we are not to be independent from God. We should become increasingly dependent upon Him in order to fulfill our destiny and His calling on our lives. We must place our anchor firmly in the waters of faith, hope and love.

I began running later in life. It's quite interesting how I used to dread the one-mile run in middle school and now I actually pay to run 5Ks, 10Ks, half marathons, and even marathons. Who would have thought?

When I run a race, I hit a dip usually at some point. It varies, but for the most part it is between the first mile and the second mile during a 5K and at mile 20 during a marathon. Likewise, I hit a dip in my life in my midforties. Everyone, at one point or another, hits a dip in their life. We all go through a time of uncertainty, trials, or struggles. You will reach the other side of this journey.

There are times that you must revisit places of hurt in order to get to the other side of the pain such as with childhood trauma. Whenever you go through trials, you just have to keep taking one step forward and then another step. It takes time, but you will get there. Just keep making forward progress. Keep striving, day by day, to get closer to God.

What does it mean to cross over to the other side?
_____
_____
_____

Oh, how we want to be on the other side! We desperately want to be on the other side of this trial, the other side of this illness, or the other side of our sinful selves. Sometimes, you just have to get out of the boat. Stop being afraid and get out of the boat like Peter did. Then, keep your eyes on Jesus. Keep your faith and trust in Him alone. We must have faith until we get there, but rest assured, we will get there. You will know you have reached the other side when it no longer feels raw like it was while going through the pain, heartache, or struggle.

A friend once told me, "Sometimes we go through things to help us become what God wants us to be." You have reached the other side when you are no longer tired or weary and the tears are no longer a constant flow. You will feel like the angels are cheering you on, the endorphins are running through your body, and you're gaining strength with each new step you take. Always remember, you are not the experiences you have gone through. You are stronger because of the things you have endured. He's refining us like pearls, and pearls are formed with repeated pressure over time. "Again, the kingdom of Heaven is like a merchant seeking fine pearls, and upon finding one pearl of great value, he went and sold all that he had, and bought it," Matthew 13:45-46 says.

For the following scriptures, write the insights you gain from them to help you get to the other side. Hide them in your heart.

Here are scriptures to help you get to the other side of this trial:

- Psalm 37:39
- Psalm 91:11-15
- Matthew 19:26
- Luke 18:27
- Romans 8:28
- 2 Corinthians 1:3-5
- Philippians 4:13
- Philippians 4:19

Here are scriptures to help you get to the other side of your illness:

- Psalm 30:2
- Psalm 103:2-4
- Psalm 107:19-22
- Isaiah 53:4-5
- Matthew 9:35
- Mark 5:34
- 2 Corinthians 12:9
- Revelation 21:4

Here are scriptures to help you get to the other side of financial problems:

- Psalm 23:1
- Malachi 3:10
- 2 Corinthians 9:8

Here are some more scriptures to help you get to the other side of your sinful self:

- Psalm 25:8-11
- Psalm 103:1-5
- Romans 8:1
- Psalm 139:1-12
- Luke 7:47
- John 13:34
- 1 John 1:7

I look forward to getting to the other side. Heaven will be a glorious place.

Identify what each of the following passages teaches you about heaven:

Genesis 1:1

_____
_____
_____

Genesis 28:17

_____
_____
_____

Psalm 19:1

_____
_____
_____

Philippians 3:20

_____
_____
_____

Revelation 4

_____
_____
_____

Through all the unknowns in life, the one thing we as Christians know without a doubt is that God will be there. He promises to never leave us or forsake us Hebrews 13:5. So in this great unknown, lean on the God who loves us the most. If you choose fear, then fear in Him only. "For as high as the heavens are above the earth, so great is His lovingkindness toward those who fear Him," Psalm 103:11 teaches us.

As the hymn "Leaning on the Everlasting Arms" says, "What a fellowship, what a joy divine, leaning on the everlasting arms; what a blessedness, what a peace is mine, leaning on the everlasting arms." Never stop leaning on the everlasting arms of God! He will see us through to the other side of our trials, circumstances and this sinful world.

> Is anyone among you suffering? Let him pray. Is anyone cheerful? Let him sing praises. (James 5:13)

My song of the day: "Head in the Fight" by Sanctus Real
Your song of the day: _____

WEEK 4 DISCUSSION

Day 1. What promises are we given when we seek first the kingdom of God?
_____
_____

Day 2. Who is the one and only in your life?
_____
_____

Day 3. What was the best gift you have ever received?
_____
_____

Day 4. In what ways is your cup overflowing with blessings?
_____
_____

Day 5. What does it mean to cross over to the other side?
_____
_____

Insights to share:
_____
_____
_____
_____

WEEK 5

Dress

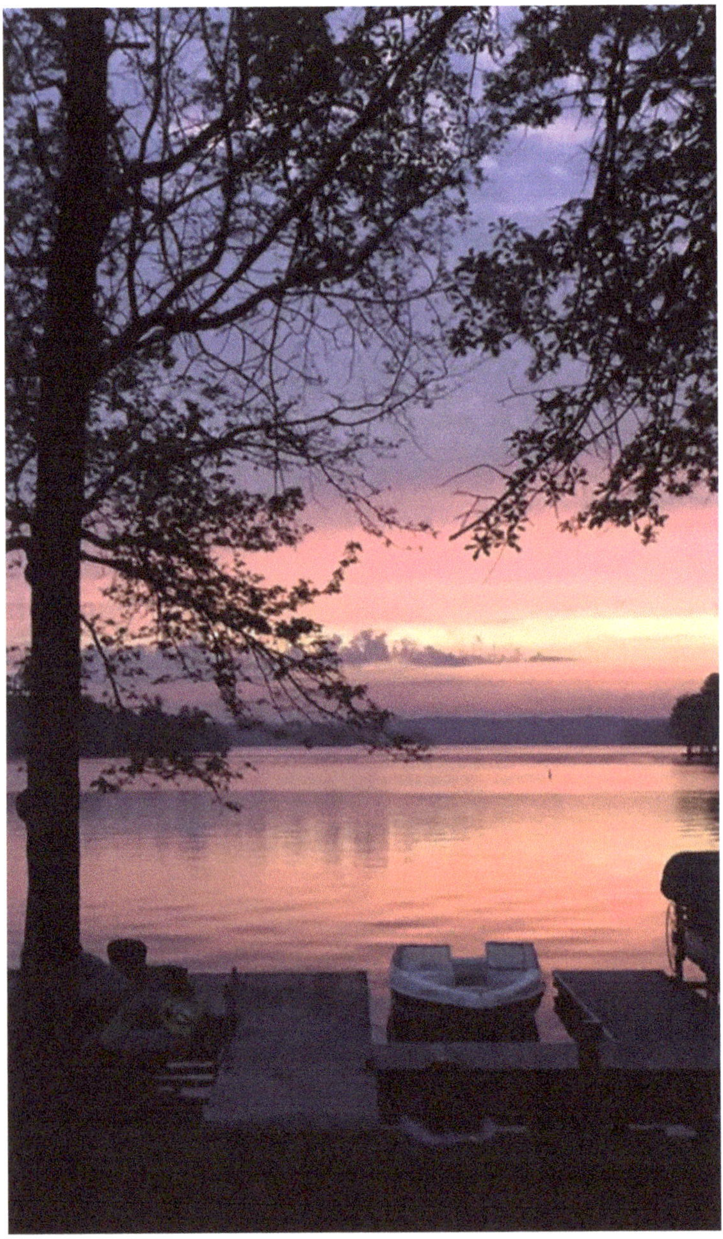

DAY 1

Dressed in His Glory

We all, with unveiled face beholding as in a mirror the glory of the Lord, are being transformed into the same image from glory to glory, just as from the Lord, the Spirit.
—2 Corinthians 3:18

How Does God Manifest His Glory?

Sunrises and sunsets are great displays of God's glory. Each one is different, and the array of colors is magnificent. I only wish pictures truly capture the splendor of them all. This is but one way that God reveals His glory. Let's take another look at John 11:40.

The word glory can be a noun or a verb.

What are the definitions of glory?

_____
_____
_____

Biblical Examples of Clothing

Write the articles of clothing or accessories mentioned in the following verses:

Genesis 3:21: _____
Genesis 41:42: _____
_____

Numbers 15:37-41: _____
_____

Esther 8:15: _____

Job 1:20: _____
Job 29:14: _____
Matthew 7:15: _____
Matthew 11:8: _____
Mark 15:17: _____
Luke 15:22: _____
_____

John 19:2: _____
_____

Revelation 3:4: _____

Read Colossians 3:12-17. As God's chosen people, what are you to clothe yourselves with? What are you to put on?
_____
_____
_____

God

Write a description of God and His Glory based on these scriptures:

Daniel 7:9: _____

Exodus 33:18-23: _____

Psalm 84:11: _____

Psalm 104:1-2: _____

Luke 2:9: _____

Read Isaiah 6:3 and fill in the missing words: "And one called to another and said, 'Holy, Holy, Holy is the Lord of hosts, the whole earth is full of His _____.'"

Jesus

Write a description of Jesus and His Glory based on these scriptures:

Psalm 8:5: _____
_____

Song of Solomon 5:10-16: _____
_____
_____

Luke 2:12: _____
Hebrews 2:7-11: _____
_____

Jude 24-25: _____
_____

Revelation 1:14: _____
_____

Revelation 19:16: _____
_____

Bride of Christ

Write a description of the Bride of Christ dressed in His Glory based on these scriptures:

Isaiah 60:1: _____
Isaiah 61:10: _____
_____

Revelation 19:7-9: _____
Psalm 103:4: _____
_____

Proverbs 12:4: _____
Proverbs 14:18: _____
Proverbs 14:24: _____
2 Corinthians 3:18: _____
Revelation 7:14: _____
_____

We all want to look our very best on our wedding day. We want to look beautiful and feel beautiful. God is the master wedding planner. Every last detail has been planned out perfectly. There are no disappointments, no snafus, no glitches. Take heed of the word in Psalm 45:10-15:

> Listen, O daughter, give attention and incline your ear; Forget your people and your father's house; Then the King will desire your beauty; because He is your Lord, bow down to Him and the daughter of Tyre will come with a gift; the rich among the people will entreat your favor. The King's daughter is all glorious within; Her clothing is interwoven with gold. She will be led to the King in embroidered work; the virgins, her companions who follow her, will be brought to Thee. They will be led forth with gladness and rejoicing; They will enter into the King's palace. (NASB)

God will transform our bodies. He will dress us up in His glory. In Philippians 3:21, it shows that God will "transform the body of our humble state into conformity with the body of His glory, by the exertion of the power that He has even to subject all things to Himself."

Read Matthew 6:13 and fill in the missing words: "And do not lead us into temptation, but deliver us from evil. For thine is the _____ and the _____ and the _____. Amen."

How does God manifest His Glory?

_____
_____
_____
_____

Glorify God

Christ cleansed ten lepers. Did anyone thank God? In Luke 17:18, it states: "Was no one found who turned back to give glory to God, except this foreigner?"

Read Colossians 3:12-17. What should God's chosen people clothe themselves with?

_____
_____
_____

JUST DIRT ON THE DRESS

Read Habakkuk 3:17-19. When should we rejoice in the Lord?

_____
_____

What does it mean to glorify God? In what ways do you glorify God?

_____
_____
_____
_____

Let us sing and shout for joy like the angels did at the birth of Jesus: "Glory to God in the highest, and on earth peace among men with whom He is pleased" (Luke 2:14). Let us do what God calls us to do.

Read 2 Corinthians 3:7-18. How are Christians transformed?

_____
_____

Read James 2:2-4. What are we not supposed to do based on someone's clothing?

_____
_____

Read Proverbs 31:24-25. How should a woman be dressed?

_____

Describe strength.

_____
_____

Describe dignity.

_____
_____

What are Christians to do according to 1 Peter 4:7-11 that will bring glory to God?

_____
_____
_____
_____

How can we glorify God in our marriages according to Ephesians 5:22-27?

_____
_____
_____

What does it take to have a strong marriage? It takes working together, communication, seeking the other's interests above your own, compromising, understanding, and seeking their perspective. Young couples are given advice at wedding showers and throughout the engagement. What advice would you give yourself? Your best friend?

Listen to what Hillsong's song "Cornerstone" has to say: "Then He shall come with trumpet sound. Oh, may I then in Him be found. Dressed in His righteousness alone. Faultless, and stand before the throne." God is transforming us for our wedding feast. He is clothing us with a heart of compassion, kindness, humility, gentleness and patience." Col 3:12

Read Revelation 19:7-10. Have you made yourself ready? How, then, are you clothed as the Bride of Christ?

_____
_____

His Robe of Righteousness dresses us in His glory. We are clothed in His fine linen, bright and clean. There are no more spots, dots, or sin stains on us. We are as white as snow.

As we close for the day, read Psalm 150 aloud and say it with true conviction. Be ready, Radiant Bride, to be clothed in His glory by the forgiveness of sins. Give Him praise forevermore for His great act of mercy and grace.

> My heart is steadfast, O God, my heart is steadfast; I will sing, yes, I will sing praises! Awake, my glory; Awake, harp and lyre, I will awaken the dawn! I will give thanks to Thee, O Lord, among the peoples; I will sing praises to Thee among the nations. For Thy lovingkindness is great to the heavens, And Thy truth to the clouds. Be exalted above the heavens, O God; Let Thy glory be above all the earth. (Ps. 57:7-11)

My song of the day: "How Great Thou Art" by Carrie Underwood
Your song of the day: _____

DAY 2

Radiant

I delight greatly in the Lord; my soul rejoices in my God. For He has clothed me with garments of salvation and arrayed me in a Robe of Righteousness, as a bridegroom adorns his head like a priest, and as a bride adorns herself with jewels.
—Isaiah 61:10

How Do You Radiate God's Love to Others?

My grandmother Reeves was a true gem! She exemplified everything a lovely lady should be: kind, sweet, dear, compassionate, helpful, always positive, and encouraging. She led by her example. She didn't tell you how many verses or chapters she read in the Bible that day; her life displayed it. She radiated with the love of Christ. Her kindness and goodness shined through. Her compliments still make their way to my thoughts when I think of her—proof that words have lasting power. Telling me that I was pretty and looked more and more like my mother are my favorite compliments.

I'm thankful that my grandmother did not see me at my heaviest. She had already gone to be with Jesus when I reached my heaviest weight of two hundred pounds and three chins. I recall looking in the mirror and being disgusted with myself. *How did I get like this?* It was as if I were sleepwalking through life eating casserole after casserole, taking the kids here and there; and finding the bagels and donuts on my thighs, hips, and the dreaded muffin top. I did not feel radiant in the least bit.

Now, I look in the mirror with new eyes, clearer eyes—with the eyes of Christ. Where I used to see double chins, beady eyes from excess facial fat, and fluffy cheeks, it suddenly became clear that it did not matter what I looked like. Jesus died for me, no matter how I looked on the outside or what I had done. Jesus loves me, and He loves you! He looks at the heart, and He knows whether or not it is open to receive His love and to follow His example.

When you look in the mirror, think of Jesus and what He did for you—*you*! Then, think of the most beautiful, radiant, and exquisite thing you can think of.

For me, an infant, especially my grandchildren, are precious and make my heart smile. Soak up that feeling when you see such a beautiful sight and tell yourself, "That's how God sees me!" His child is what He sees—beautiful, exquisite, radiant, flawless, and blameless! You sparkle and shine!

God's Brilliance

Read Genesis 1:3-5. What is the absence of darkness? How did God describe the light?

_____
_____

Read Habakkuk 3:3-4. How is the radiance of God described in this passage of scripture?

_____
_____

Read Daniel 2:20-23. God reveals the meaning of Nebuchadnezzar's dream to Daniel. What is the interpretation of the dream?

_____
_____
_____

Read Acts 12:7. How did God display His light in this passage of scripture?

_____
_____

Read 2 Corinthians 4:6. What is displayed in the face of Christ?

_____
_____

Read Revelation 21:23. What will provide light in Heaven?

_____
_____

Jesus Shines

Read Matthew 17:2. Describe Jesus's appearance?
_____
_____

Read John 8:12. What is Jesus described as in John 8:12? What does it mean to have the light of life?
_____
_____
_____
_____

Read John 1:4-5. How is Jesus described in John 1:4-5?
_____
_____

Read 1 John 1: 7. How are we to walk?
_____

Give examples of what walking in the light looks like:
_____
_____
_____
_____
_____

Is there an area of your life or something mentioned above that you currently are not doing that you would like to begin doing to walk in the light for Jesus?
_____
_____

Read John 11:10. What happens when the light is not in you? How can you keep from stumbling?
_____
_____
_____

Read John 1:1-5 and fill in the missing words:

In the beginning was the _____, and the _____ was with God, and the _____ was God. He was in the beginning with God. All things came into being by Him, and apart from Him nothing came into being that has come into being. In Him was life, and the life was the _____ of men. And the _____ shines in the darkness and the darkness did not comprehend it.

Read Revelation 1:9-18. Write a description of Jesus based on Revelation 1:12-16.
_____
_____
_____

The Family Man is one of my favorite movies, one of the few that I can watch over and over. The leading man is given a glimpse of what his life would have been like had he taken another road in life. Instead of seeking wealth and prestige, what if he had taken the route that included staying with the lady he loved and making a life with her. He is suddenly thrown into a middle-class life with two children.

In one of my favorite scenes, he truly gets a look at Kate, his "wife," and sees her as the beautiful lady that she is. The way he looks into her eyes and says, "You're beautiful. You're really stunning. You've really grown into a beautiful woman." Of course, Kate is baffled as to how he can look at her as if he hadn't seen her for the past thirteen years. Isn't that how we want to be looked at? Whether or not anyone does that here on earth, just know in your heart that God looks at you with tenderness and the greatest amount of love possible because God is love.

It truly is amazing to see how God answers even what appears to me to be such an insignificant prayer request such as wanting to feel loved. He cares about every detail of your life and that includes feeling radiant and beautiful from time to time. Allow God to fill any emptiness you may be feeling. Pray about it, and God will fill you up with more than you even ask.

Read Psalm 34:4-5. What happens when you look to God?
_____
_____

I love the holidays! Trees and buildings lit up with twinkling lights just makes me smile. Something as simple as lights can literally brighten your day and put a smile on your face. We are the light of the world through Jesus. Share your light each and every day.

What Is Our Identity in Christ?

A Radiant Life

Read the following scriptures and write the insights you gain regarding having a radiant life

Psalm 18:28: _____
Psalm 27:1: _____
Psalm 34:5: _____
Psalm 36:9: _____
Psalm 37:6: _____
Psalm 56:13: _____
Psalm 80:3: _____
Psalm 89:15: _____
Psalm 97:11: _____
Psalm 118:27: _____
Psalm 119:105: _____
Psalm 119:130: _____

A Radiant Bride

Read Proverbs 4:7-9. When you as a Christian gain wisdom, how are you adorned?

_____
_____

Daniel 12:3 states, "And those who have insight will shine brightly like the brightness of the expanse of heaven, and those who lead the many to righteousness, like the stars forever and ever." Be one of those who have insight, Radiant Bride of Christ! You be the candelabras and the unity candle as you are united with Christ. Share His light to the world.

Continue to seek and grow in the knowledge of our Lord and Savior Jesus Christ. When we seek after Him, we radiate His light and love all around us. We become more radiant than a bride in her wedding dress adorned with makeup and jewelry. There will be a day when we will be presented with a glorious crown. Can you picture it?

Read 1 Corinthians 15:42-44. Write the opposite for each of the following:

Perishable body _____
Sown in Dishonor _____
Sown in weakness _____
Sown a natural body _____

According to 1 Corinthians 15:52, what will happen to us in the "twinkling of an eye at the last trumpet?"
Read Hebrews 1:3-4 and fill in the missing words:

And He is the _____ of His _____ and the exact representation of His nature, and upholds all things by the word of His _____. When He had made purification of sins, He sat down at the right hand of the _____ on _____.

Read 1 Peter 2:9 and fill in the missing words:

But you are a chosen race, a royal priesthood, a holy nation, a people for God's own possession that you may proclaim the excellencies of _____ who has called you out of _____ into _____ _____ _____.

Read 1 John 1:5 and fill in the missing words:

"And this is the message we have heard from Him and announce to you, **that** _____ is _____, and in _____ there is _____ darkness at all."

Guidance

What insights do you gain about how God guides His people?

Psalm 78:14: _____
Psalm 4:6: _____
Isaiah 42:6: _____

Psalm 16:7-8: _____
Psalm 25:4-5: _____
Psalm 143:8: _____
Jeremiah 29:11 _____

Shine the Light

Read John 1:6-9. Who shined the light of Jesus? _____

What do the following scriptures say about light?

Jeremiah 31:12: _____
Matthew 5:14-16: _____
_____
Matthew 10:27: _____
John 5:35: _____
Ephesians 5:8-17: _____
_____
Hebrews 1:3: _____
1 Peter 3:3-4: _____
Revelation 7:14: _____
Revelation 21:23-24: _____
_____

How do you radiate God's love to others?
_____
_____
_____

A simple smile can light up the room. Our light will never extinguish if we put our faith and hope in Jesus. In John 11:25, Jesus tells Martha, "I am the resurrection and the life; he who believes in Me shall live even if he dies." Get ready for Jesus by not putting on jewels, adorning yourself in a beautiful dress, makeup, etc., get ready for Jesus with your gentle and quiet spirit, which is pleasing to God. Jesus gives you the crown of life. Always be ready. Revelation 3:11 states, "I am coming quickly, hold fast what you have, in order that no one take your crown."

For many years, I did not really see the world as I do now. You see, when you live with shame, you do not always look up at people. You don't always look into people's eyes, and you smile less. How things are different when you accept yourself as God sees you, the Radiant Bride that you are. When you walk with the radiance of God, you shine His glory wherever you go! Shine for Him! Look at people and greet them with a smile. Smiles are contagious, and it spreads joy wherever you go.

Remember what Ephesians 5:18b-19 says: "But be filled with the Spirit, speaking to one another in psalms and hymns and spiritual songs, singing and making melody with your heart to the Lord."

My song of the day: "This Little Light of Mine" by Odetta
Your song of the day: _____

DAY 3

Exquisite

The Lord your God is with you, he is mighty to save. He will take great delight in you, he will quiet you with His love, He will rejoice over you with singing.
—Zephaniah 3:17

How Does God See Each of Us?

I pray that you were raised in such a way that you feel good about yourself. Many things in life can damage our outlook on ourselves. There's nothing more harmful than growing up with shame. It's as if the bullies of the world can sense it, which heightens the downfall of one's self-worth. When we keep our eyes on Jesus, we keep our perspective of ourselves in balance. It doesn't tilt too much to the side of low self-esteem or too far to the other side of thinking too highly of ourselves. Keep yourself in balance by picturing Jesus on the cross for each of us.

I'm thankful that God gives each of us special relationships called friendship. I have been extremely blessed with many amazing friends over the years—from the friend who's been with me since we were six years old to the one I met last week and all of the ones in between. They have richly blessed my life, and I can only hope that I have made a difference in their lives. It is not by coincidence that our paths crossed. I truly believe that God has a purpose for each acquaintance and each friendship He places in our lives. When you ponder all of the places some friends traveled before landing in your lives, it truly makes you realize how God orchestrates it all for our good. There could be something that we need to learn from each other or perhaps help each other through a difficult season in life. Some were once my teachers who turned into lasting friendships. Some friendships are there just for pure joy and to help each other laugh along the way. All of these friends have come in different packages with a wide variety of personalities and at various times in my life. Each one has made a lasting imprint on my life.

Perhaps all the data collection I do as a teacher inspired me to do a little data on myself. After the death of my class valedictorian, I was curious to see what she had written to me thirty years ago in my yearbook. Then, I began reading everyone's comments and putting tally marks under the reoccurring themes.

The majority of the comments were wishing me good luck or best wishes in the future whether it involved just the summer or beyond. The next popular comments were about how sweet or nice I was, for being understanding even when we had differences, and how fun I was to be around. Sometimes, I'm curious how others see me because I'm hoping that my life reflects that of a Christian. The problem arises when I'm too concerned with how others view me. What's most important is how God sees me.

How does God see each of us?

___

This quote from Beth Moore's *Breaking Free* hit me between the eyes:

> I always viewed myself as a big spot on a white dress—a spot that everyone saw and pointed at in disgust. I thought everyone was beautiful in God's sight but me. At a wedding, I watched in awe as the stunning bride walked down the aisle. God whispered to my heart, "That's how I see you." I can't begin to tell you how free I am! I no longer feel dirty or spotted with guilt. I am a true child of God—without spot.

Read Psalm 139:13-15. How did God make each of us?

___

I take great delight in teaching and being around children. They are so innocent and tell you just what they are thinking. They haven't developed a filter yet; therefore, they are completely honest. In my current position at school, I have the opportunity to teach some of the same children for several years.

In spring 2013, I read a *Fancy Nancy* book titled *Bonjour, Butterfly*. It is a story about a little girl who loves butterflies. Fancy Nancy is in the process of helping her best friend plan a butterfly-themed birthday party with butterfly invitations, decorations, and all. To her dismay, the party is scheduled the same day as her grandparent's fiftieth wedding anniversary in Paris, France. She is heartbroken to have to miss her best friend's party.

It is a great story about friendship and love. What makes this book extra special to me is the use of fancy words that students might not otherwise come across at such a young age. Some of the fancy words in this book are *extraordinary, glamorous, gorgeous,* and thrilled. The one that I like best is *exquisite*. It is probably my favorite because it was the first word that a student used the next day and then periodically ever since to describe me. It just makes my heart smile when my students come into my classroom and say, "Mrs. Shumpert, you look exquisite!" I, in turn, use the different words to describe my students to give them the same joy that they give me.

Make a list of people or things you find exquisite.

That's exactly how God sees us. We were made in His image, remember? To God, we are exquisite, gorgeous, and extraordinary. Can you hear Him telling you that? Close your eyes and imagine God speaking words of exultation over you. Feel His adoration for you.

What would God say about your heart, your inward beauty?

_____
_____
_____

Would He say, there's a spot? Let me clean it up for you. Do you need to ask Him to point out the stains which are the sins you are not yet aware of?

What song would God sing to you? _____
What songs are you missing because you are just too busy to listen?

_____
_____

How can you see the visible prints of an invisible God?

_____
_____
_____

> And let not your adornment be merely external—braiding the hair,
> and wearing gold jewelry, or putting on dresses; but let it be the hidden

person of the heart, with the imperishable quality of a gentle and quiet spirit, which is precious in the sight of God" (1 Pet. 3:3-4).

Read Proverbs 31:25 and fill in the missing blanks: "_____ and _____ are her clothing. And she _____ at the future."

Wear your crown. Don't give it away. You are a child of the Almighty God (Rev. 3:11). Don't take off your crown. Keep being your best.

Fill in the missing words from Revelations 3:4-5 (NIV):

Yet you have a few people in Sardis who have not _____ their _____. They will _____ with me, _____ in _____, for they are _____. The one who is _____ will, like them, be _____ in _____. I will never _____ out the name of that person from the _____ of _____, but will acknowledge that name before my _____, and his angels. Whoever has ears, let them hear what the _____ says to the churches.

God's Word is filled with His feelings for you and me. He loves His exquisite bride. Song of Solomon 4:9-10a says, "You have stolen my heart, my sister, my bride; you have stolen my heart with one glance of your eyes, with one jewel of your necklace. How delightful is your love, my sister, my bride!"

Alternatively, Song of Solomon 7:5-6 also says, "Your head crowns you like Mount Carmel. Your hair is like royal tapestry; the king is held captive by its tresses. How beautiful you are and how pleasing, my love with your delights!"

I would like to close today's lesson with the words from Song of Solomon 4:1-8a:

How beautiful you are, my darling! Oh, how beautiful! Your eyes behind your veil are doves. Your hair is like a flock of goats descending from the hills of Gilead. Your teeth are like a flock of sheep just shorn, coming up from the washing. Each has its twin; not one of them is alone. Your lips are like a scarlet ribbon; your mouth is lovely. Your temples behind your veil are like the halves of a pomegranate. Your neck is like the tower of David, built with courses of stone; on it hang a thousand shields, all of them shields of warriors. Your breasts are like two fawns, like twin fawns of a gazelle that browse among the lilies. Until the day breaks and the shadows flee, I will go to the mountain of myrrh and to the hill of incense. You are altogether beautiful, my darling; there is no flaw in you. Come with me from Lebanon, my bride, come with me from Lebanon.

Believe—truly believe—the love and adoration your God has for you and remember to "sing praises to God, sing praises; Sing praises to our King, sing praises" (Ps. 47:6).

My song of the day: "Wedding Day" by Casting Crowns
Your song of the day: _____

DAY 4

Song of Solomon

I am my beloved and my beloved is mine.
—Song of Solomon 6:3

How Does Song of Solomon Show You God's Adoration for You?

Of all the gifts a person could have, a beautiful singing voice would be what I would choose. To be able to belt it out like Carrie Underwood would be the ultimate feeling. Oh, how I want to sing to my beloved Jesus! Certainly, I am grateful to be able to sing, and it is a sin to be envious of another one's gift; therefore, I gladly make a joyful noise singing praises to our King. I'm pretty sure that by the time my words float to heaven, my song has been transformed into something angelic. God has given me other gifts; therefore, I use them to tell Him of my great love for Him.

J. Vernon McGee says,

> The Song of Solomon is 1 of 1,005 songs written by Solomon. To put it in perspective, Solomon wrote at least 1,005 days if he wrote a song each day, which is a total of more than 2 years of writing songs in his lifetime, not to mention the over 3,000 proverbs he wrote. He was quite the writer. Song of Solomon is not a story but a song to encourage the Bride of Christ to have a close relationship with our Lord and Savior; our Beloved.

How does God romance you? There are many ways that God romances me: gorgeous sunrises, sunsets, special shaped clouds, butterfly kisses, peace, encouraging words, music, and many others. An overwhelming sense of His presence is by far the best way He romances me. One day last fall, I went out in the yard and picked flowers from my azalea bush and placed them in a vase. The next day, I noticed several of the red leaves had fallen onto the counter. It was fascinating to see so many arranged in the shapes of hearts. To me, it was a romantic gift from God. Love poured into my heart that day.

God leaves His love notes for us wherever we look for them. Song of Solomon is His love note to us. Getting notes, especially notes of admiration, are so much fun to receive. Don't you agree? The spoken word is powerful, but there is just something about the written word that makes it that much more meaningful and special. Perhaps, the reason is you can go back to it and savor it over and over. Let's savor the word of God by studying scriptures daily.

Wedding Procession

Read Psalm 45:10-15. How will the bride be brought to the King?
_____
_____
_____

Read Song of Songs 3:6-11. Draw a picture of how you picture these verses.

Come Along

Fill in the missing words from the following scriptures:

Song of Solomon 1:4—"Draw me after you and let us _____ together!"
Song of Solomon 1:4—"The king has _____ me into His chambers."
Song of Solomon 1:8—"_____ _____ on the trail of the flock."
Song of Solomon 2:4—"He has _____ me to His banquet hall."
Song of Solomon 2:8—"Listen! My beloved! Behold, He is _____, _____ on the mountains, _____ on the hills!"
Song of Solomon 2:10—"My beloved responded and said to me, _____, my darling, my beautiful one, and _____ _____."

The following are a list of verbs used in Song of Solomon (NASB). Highlight the words used that remind you of the love Jesus has for you. Now, this is your chance to doodle. I'll allow it this time. Draw a symbol or jot down a phrase to help cement these thoughts into your mind. Don't ever forget the great love that Jesus has for you!

- Kiss
- Love/loves
- Draw me
- Run
- Sustain me
- Refresh me
- Embrace me (with his right hand and his left hand under my head)
- Rejoice
- Extol
- Adjure
- Awaken
- Listen/listening
- Behold
- Climbing
- Leaping
- Standing
- Looking
- Peering
- Responded
- Arise
- Come
- Appeared
- Arrived
- Hear/has heard
- Ripened
- See/sought/seek/seen
- Catch
- Pastures
- Found
- Held
- Conceived
- Perfumed
- Guarding
- Gaze
- Drip
- Locked/sealed
- Flowing
- Gather/gathered
- Eaten

- Drink
- Captivated
- Leaning

Perhaps I'm showing my age with this next story, but I must tell you that Pond's Cold Cream reminds me of summer. My mom would lather us in it when we would inevitably get sunburned. Whenever I get a sniff of that smell, it automatically takes me back to those summers long ago. Today, we would most likely say we use aloe, which is what I used on my children. I tell you this, not to reveal my true age but to get you thinking about what certain smells remind you of. Pine reminds me of Christmas.

Read Song of Solomon 1:3.

When my husband is out of town on business, I sleep in one of his shirts. His scent while I'm sleeping is comforting; however, it pales in comparison to the comfort I receive from our Savior, Jesus. Just saying the name of Jesus is like the most beautiful scent poured out. The following scents were mentioned in Song of Solomon. Oh, how I wish this were a Scratch 'N Sniff book at the moment. Then, you would be able to sample all of the aromas mentioned.

- Pleasing
- Purified oil (fragrance of oils)
- Pouch of myrrh
- Cluster of Henna Blossoms
- Fragrance from vines in blossom
- Lilies
- Frankincense
- Scented powders
- Sedan chair for King Solomon
- Timber of Lebanon (fragrance of Lebanon)
- Fragrance of your garments
- Spices
- Honey
- Orchard of pomegranates
- Nard
- Saffron
- Calamus
- Cinnamon

- Aloes
- Garden spring
- Fresh water
- Balsam
- Sweet-scented herbs
- Apples (fragrance of your breath)

Read Ephesians 5:1-2. How is Christ described in these verses?
_____

Read 2 Corinthians 2:15-16. What are we to God? _____
Read Romans 5:5 and Song of Songs 4:7. How does God see each of us?
_____
_____

Have you taken care of your vineyard? A summer tan makes me happy. I enjoy wearing skirts and dresses much more with a nice tan. The tans over the years, however, have produced age spots on me, particularly my arms. These blemishes are signs of overexposure to the sun's UV rays. Likewise, too much exposure to worldly things will blemish your soul. Take care of your vineyard and your soul by staying in God's Word. A daily dose of His word will do wonders!

Being extremely nearsighted as a child came with hindrances. Being filled with the spirit of God and experiencing His love for me is comparable to the first time of being able to see clearly after corrective eye surgery. I now see for the first time how much He cares for me. I'm no longer blind to the fact that He only loves the perfect ones, the beautiful ones, the outgoing ones. Jesus loves me. This I do know, and the Bible reminds us in these verses: "His banner over me is love" (Sg 2:4) and "He calls me beautiful one" (Sg 2:10).

Read Song of Songs 1:15, 2:4, 2:10 and answer the following questions:
How does Song of Solomon show you God's adoration for you?
_____
_____

How are Jesus and the Bride described in the following verses?
_____
_____

JUST DIRT ON THE DRESS

Jot the descriptors down in Song of Solomon 1:15-16 in the appropriate columns below:

        Jesus   Bride

I had the great pleasure of being at my parents' house when a special package was delivered from my aunt. Inside the package were letters from my grandfather to my grandmother while they were courting in 1944. One was written two years prior to what would be my mom's birthday. In each letter were nicknames for one another such as my darling and my dearest darling.

What are your nicknames given to you by your Beloved (Jesus)?
_____
_____

What things are the Bride of Christ compared to with Jesus?
_____
_____

Fill in the missing words in the scriptures below:

    For your love is better than _____. (Song of Sol. 1:2)

    Your name is like _____. (Song of Sol. 1:3)

    To me, my darling, you are like _____ _____ among the _____ of Pharaoh. (Song of Sol. 1:9)

    Your _____ are _____ with _____, your neck with _____ _____ _____. (Song of Sol. 1:10)

    My beloved is to me a _____ ____ _____ which lies all night between my breasts. (Song of Sol. 1:13)

My beloved is to me a _____ __ _____ _____ in the _____ of Engedi. (Song of Sol. 1:14)

How _____ you are, my beloved, and so _____! Indeed, our couch is luxuriant. The beams of our houses are _____, our rafters, _____. (Sg 1:16-17)

Like an _____ _____ among the trees of the forest, so is my beloved among the young men. (Sg 2:3)

My beloved is like a _____ or a _____ _____. (Sg 2:9)

Fill in the missing words used to describe the Bride in these scriptures:

I am black but _____. (Sg 1:5)

_____ _____ among women. (Sg 1:8)

How _____ you are, my _____, How _____ you are! Your eyes are like _____. (Sg 1:15)

Like a _____ among the thorns, so is my _____ among the maidens. (Sg 2:2)

How _____ you are, my darling, How _____ you are! Your _____ are like _____ behind your veil; Your _____ is like a _____ of _____ that have descended from Mount Gilead. (Sg 4:1)

Your _____ are like a _____ of newly shorn _____ which have come up from their washing, all of which bear twins, and not one among them has lost her young. (Sg 4:2)

Your _____ are like a _____ _____, and your _____ is _____. Your _____ are like a _____ of a _____ behind your veil. (Sg 4:3)

JUST DIRT ON THE DRESS

Your _____ is like the _____ of David built with rows of stones, on which are hung a thousand shields, all the round shields of the mighty men. (Sg 4:4)

Your _____ _____ are like _____ _____, twins of a Gazelle, which feed among the lilies. (Sg 4:5)

You are _____ _____, my _____, and there in no blemish in you. (Sg 4:7)

You are as _____ as Tirzah, my darling, as _____ as _____, as _____ as an _____ with _____. (Sg 6:4)

But my _____, my _____ _____ is _____. (Sg 6:9)

The maidens saw her and called her _____. (Sg 6:9d)

Fill in the missing words describing Jesus Christ in these scriptures:

My beloved is _____ and _____, _____ among ten thousand. (Sg 5:10)

His _____ is like _____, _____ _____. His _____ are like _____ of _____, and black as a _____. (Sg 5:11)

His _____ are like _____, beside streams of water, bathed in milk, and reposed in their setting. (Sg 5:12)

How was Jesus described in Matthew 28:3?

_____
_____

Your love Jesus is better than wine, chocolate, accolades, money, gifts, things, or anything this world has to offer. You, Jesus, are my SOS (Song of Solomon), my Beloved, my everything!

Remember Song of Solomon 3:3-4:

> The watchmen found me as they made their rounds in the city. 'Have you seen the one my heart loves?' Scarcely had I passed them when I found the one my heart loves. I held him and would not let Him go till I had brought Him to my mother's house, to the room of the one who conceived me.

> I will sing to the Lord as long as I live; I will sing praise to my God while I have my being. (Ps. 104:33)

My song of the day: Canon in D Major by Johann Pachelbel
Your song of the day: _____

DAY 5

Saved, Sanctified, and Set Free

Now may the God of peace Himself sanctify you entirely; and may your spirit and soul and body be preserved complete, without blame at the coming of our Lord Jesus Christ.
—1 Thessalonians 5:23

What Does It Mean to You to Truly Be Set Free?

I sometimes wonder what it would feel like to jump out of an airplane. I'm pretty sure someone would actually have to push me out. My dad was a paratrooper in the service during the Vietnam War Era from 1962 to 1968. Oftentimes, I have wondered how on earth he was able to make himself jump out of a perfectly good airplane. How do you get past the fear of taking that leap of faith? But once you get past that fear, there must be a sense of freedom as you are making your way from the clouds to the ground.

Sometimes you have to be willing to jump before God will allow you to soar. We must jump at times to be in accordance with God's will. He wants us to take a leap of faith!

I try to envision the woman going through this Bible study that God placed on my heart and into your hands. Is it a young, engaged twenty-year-old woman; someone in their forties; or an older woman? Regardless your age, where you've been or what you've done, God wants the same for each of us: He wants us to be saved, sanctified, and set free!

Saved

Go back to the first question from day 1 of our Bible study. Why did God provide a way of salvation?

God provides a way for each of us to be blameless through Jesus's sacrifice in order that we can meet Him in the sky on His great return. Do you ever try to picture that in your mind of just how awesome that will be?

We thank you, Lord, that we get to be your princess and be a part of the Bride of Christ—not because of what we do but because of what Jesus did for each of us. He alone washes away our dirt, grime, sins, and stains. Jesus makes us worthy to live in the heavenly realms as His beautiful, radiant, and exquisite bride, His beloved, as said in Matthew 10:39: "He who has found his life shall lose it, and he who has lost his life for My sake shall find it."

Read Luke 17:33 and fill in the missing words: "Whoever _____ to keep _____ life shall _____ it, and whoever _____ _____ life shall _____ it."

Read 1 John 2:1-2 and fill in the missing words:

My little children, I am writing these things to ____ that _____ may not sin. And if _____ sins, we have an _____ with the Father, _____ _____ the righteous; and He Himself is the _____ for _____ sins; and not _____ only, but also for those of the _____ _____.

"Just living is not enough, said the butterfly. One must have sunshine, freedom and a little flower," as Hans Christian Andersen put it. Our sunshine is Jesus, and He offers us freedom. The little flower that provides our nourishment is the Word of God. Since Jesus is the Word of God, He's all we need to have freedom.

God allowed me the privilege of saving a painted lady butterfly. It was trapped underneath the lid of a hummingbird feeder. Movement from the feeder caught my attention (of course, at a time when I could not immediately go rescue it). After taking it out of the hummingbird feeder (well, the water jostled and she fell out), I held the beautiful butterfly for about fifteen minutes to allow the wings to dry. It was a thrilling feeling to be able to hold the beautiful butterfly for so long talking to it and willing it to be okay. Then, I carefully placed it on the lantanas where it liked to get its nourishment. The wings started to move up and down. Next thing I know, it took off in my direction; however, it landed back on the ground. She took a walk across my foot and the grassy area until the wet, sticky wings were dry enough for her to take off and, oh, did she take off. She went up above the school building into the clouds as far as the eye could see. She was free, and I was given the privilege to help make her free. What a blessing!

Sanctified

Read Hebrews 2:11. What are we called by Jesus?
_____

Read 1 Corinthians 1:30. What did Jesus become to those of us who accept His salvation?
_____
_____

What three things can we claim when we are in Christ Jesus?

-
-
-

Read 1 Corinthians 6:9-11. Who will not inherit the kingdom of God?
_____

What are some examples of wrongdoers?
_____
_____
_____
_____

In the name of Jesus Christ and by the Spirit of our God, what are we as Christians?

-
-
-

Read 1 Peter 1:1-5. What hope is given in these verses?
_____
_____

Read 1 Peter 3:15. Do you have your speech ready in order "to give an account for the hope that is in you?" Write it here:

_____
_____
_____
_____
_____

Free

You get a different perspective when traveling in an airplane. A bird's-eye view is what people call it. Currently, I have flown only three round trips in my life. The view is spectacular! The sun glistens off the bodies of water. The clouds can be thick or thin, puffy or stretched out, close together, or spread apart like little cotton balls placed near the ground in no particular order. At times, the view is over beautiful bodies of water. While at other times, you see clusters of houses, buildings, businesses, or open land with many trees. You are so far off the ground that it can be unsettling for the infrequent flyer.

At times, God calls you to have that "jumping out of an airplane" moment in order to be free. He may ask you to do the hard thing or the thing you really do not want to do because it will lead to your freedom. Your leap of faith could be to have that hard conversation with someone, go to another job location, quit your job to do ministry work, or any number of things. The key is to have trust in God that He is right there with you. Be sure to pray about each and every decision. Then, live in your freedom by abiding in God's will for your life and know for certain that He is already working it out for your good.

Read Proverbs 11:21. Compare and contrast the consequences of the wicked and the righteous.

_____
_____

Read John 8:31-36. Write verse 36 in the space provided and on the tablet of your heart.

_____
_____
_____

What is everyone a slave to without Jesus? _____

Read John 8:32 and fill in the missing words: "Then you will know the _____, and the _____ will set you _____."

Read Galatians 5:13. What are we to do with our freedom?
_____

Read 1 Corinthians 6:14.

He will raise us up. We may fly low to the ground at first, but we're flying. He will raise us up higher and higher as our faith in Him grows. Listen to one of the many artists who sing "You Raise Me Up" (Josh Groban, Westlife, etc.) and read Ephesians 3:16-19.

Radiant Bride, truly be free in the knowledge that you are loved! Turn these scriptures into a prayer for yourself and others.

Get Ready to SOAR…

Seeking a heart that loves Him and His Word
Obedience
Accepting His Will and
Radiate His Love wherever you go

Get busy, Radiant Bride, to seek, obey, accept and radiate.

Read 2 Corinthians 3:16-18 and summarize these verses:
_____
_____
_____

Fill in the missing words in John 8:36: "If therefore the Son shall make you ____, you shall be ____ indeed."

Read Revelation 22:17. Will you take the free gift of the water of life? _____
Then, all you need to do is _____.

Read Revelation 22:20-21. Make a list of the strongholds from which you have been set free.

Pray about the strongholds you are still grappling with. List them and pray about them daily.

Read Isaiah 55:12. What feelings arise when reading this verse? What does it truly mean to be set free?
_____
_____
_____

Read Psalm 16:11. The Bible urges us to be

> free from strongholds,
> released from guilt,
> exempted or emancipated,
> elated,
> delivered,
> obedient, and
> made new.

Thank you, Lord, for leading me down your path for my life. I have the assurance that you will be with me and there is pure joy in your presence. I anxiously await the pleasures and treasures you bring my way. I'll be on the lookout for them.

We have come full circle like a wedding ring. Each of us were fearfully and wonderfully made without blemish, pure, and blameless. We have a way of messing that up and becoming stained with sin; however, through Jesus we are made worthy to live in the heavenly realms with Him. We come back to the place where we are again without blemish, pure, and blameless because of the blood of Jesus. He makes us worthy to be a part of the Bride of Christ. Because of Him, we have hope and freedom! Put on your crown of life, dear Bride.

> Remember: HOPE
> Heavenly Home
> Of
> People who accept the free gift of salvation for
> Eternity

We are eternally thankful for our Lord and Savior, Jesus Christ!

My greatest joy on earth has been to be a wife, mother, and now a grandmother; but all these pale in comparison to being free in Christ. Living with Him in Heaven will be the greatest joy of all!

God is the master wedding planner. Every last detail has been planned out perfectly. There are no disappointments, no rain, no snafus, no glitches. He tells Jesus at just the right time to go get your Bride. Be ready, Radiant Bride of Christ!

The Bride of Christ

> The church is the Bride of Christ,
> and you can be a part of it too.
> I came just as I am

because I want to be just with God.
He treats me just as if I've never sinned.
What kind of Justice is that?
He justifies me and all who wants to be.
Dirt was splattered on me.
It's Just Dirt on the Dress
Jesus cleans up all the mess!
He removes the dirt, sin, and stains.
washes us as white as snow,
blots out all our iniquities—
this I do know.
Then, we can influence others to do the same
to be renewed, restored, and to put on that Robe of Righteousness,
like a Butterfly goes through a metamorphosis.
So take hold of your part of the Tree of Life,
give Jesus your yoke of slavery,
and Yearn to Learn His Word.
But you better be on guard!
Stand on Christ the Solid Rock—
look out for His blessings, God winks, and moments!
Then, you will be on cloud nine with Jesus.
March onward, Christian Soldier!
The Jesus is Thy Lord, and you shall be free!
Jesus is the One and Only, the Indescribable Gift, and our Good Shepherd
who wants us to get to the other side called Heaven,
dressed in His Glory, radiant and exquisite,
like the Beloved in Song of Solomon—
saved, sanctified, and set free for all eternity!

Now, let's make it personalized for you:

    I am a part of the Bride of Christ. I came just as I am because I want to be just with God. He treats me just as if I've never sinned. He treats me just as if I've never _____, _____, or _____. What kind of justice is that? Jesus is perfect. Yet, He justifies me and all who wants to be. Dirt was splattered on me such as _____, _____, and _____. But it's just dirt on the dress. Jesus cleans up all the mess. He removes the dirt, sin, and stains. He washes me as white as snow. Blots out all my iniquities. This I do know. Then, we can influence others to do the same. I can influence _____, _____, and _____, as well as countless others that come in my path. I am renewed, restored, and I get to wear that Robe of Righteousness. It's like a butterfly that goes through a metamorphosis. I will take hold of my part of the tree of life. I give Jesus my yoke of slavery such as _____, _____, and _____. I yearn to learn His word. I will be on guard and stand on Christ the solid rock! I will continue to look for His blessings, Godwinks and moments. Today, I found _____, _____, and _____. I am on cloud nine with Jesus! March onward, Christian Soldier! The Jesus is thy Lord, and you shall be free! Jesus is the One and Only, the Indescribable Gift, and our Good Shepherd who wants me to get to the other side called heaven, dressed in His Glory, radiant and exquisite, like the Beloved in Song of Solomon. _____, you are saved, sanctified, and set free for all Eternity!

In order to soar and find freedom, you must allow God to tend to your soul, spirit, and mind. You cannot soar if you worry. You cannot soar if you are afraid. You cannot soar if you never try. Get out of your nest and fly! Don't be like the bird who is trapped inside the airport. Be free—be free like a leaf blowing in the wind on a blustery autumn day going in the direction that God has chosen for you. Remember, your life is His story in the making. Allow God to reveal to you the very next step to take for His glory!

By the power given by the Almighty Heavenly Father, I pronounce you the Bride of Christ. You may run into the arms of Jesus.

My song of the day: "Even so Come" by Chris Tomlin
Your song of the day: _____

In Christ, we have freedom!

WEEK 5 DISCUSSION

Day 1. How does God manifest His glory?

Day 2. How do you radiate God's love to others?

Day 3. How does God see each of us?

Day 4. How does Song of Solomon show you God's adoration for you?

Day 5. What does it mean to you to truly be set free?

Insights to share or questions to ask the group:

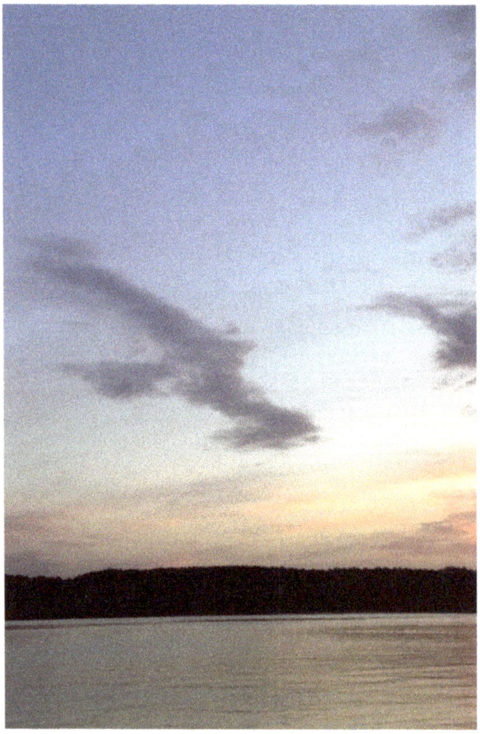

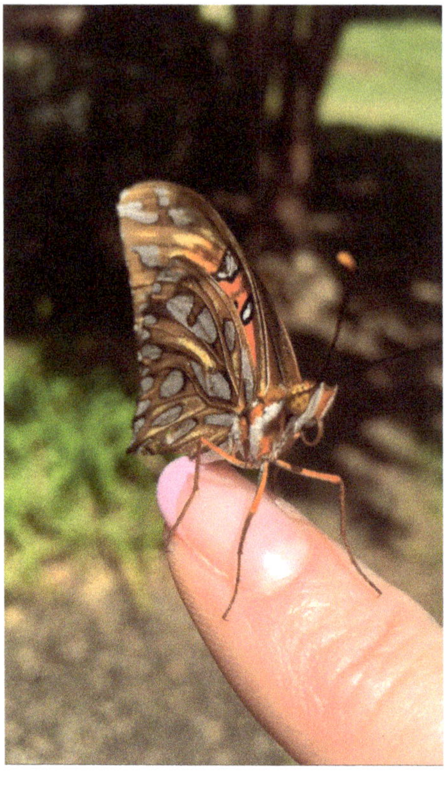

REFERENCES

Adamfulgence. "ODETTA - This Little Light of Mine -." YouTube. March 11, 2013. Accessed June 15, 2017. http://www.youtube.com/watch?v=J2kDsqGeoLU.

Allansantosh. "Cornerstone - Cornerstone - Hillsong Live 2012 - (HD) (With Lyrics)." YouTube. July 12, 2012. Accessed June 15, 2017. http://www.youtube.com/watch?v=QvLxZEU02uI.

Allen, David Lewis, and R. Kent Hughes. 1-3 John: fellowship in Gods family. Wheaton, IL: Crossway, 2013.

Alwaysforgiven821. "Amazing Grace (My Chains are Gone) - Chris Tomlin (with lyrics)." YouTube. February 25, 2008. Accessed June 15, 2017. http://www.youtube.com/watch?v=Jbe7OruLk8I.

Andersen, H. C. Hans Christian Anderson: the complete fairy tales. Ware, U.K.: Wordsworth Editions, 2009.

Bass, Ellen, and Laura Davis. The courage to heal: a guide for women survivors of child sexual abuse. New York: Collins Living, 2008.

BDWmusic. "Big Daddy Weave - Overwhelmed [Official Music Video]." YouTube. August 07, 2014. Accessed June 15, 2017. http://www.youtube.com/watch?v=BiGb14tTaH4.

BDWmusic. "Big Daddy Weave - "Redeemed" (Official Music Video)." YouTube. May 03, 2012. Accessed June 15, 2017. http://www.youtube.com/watch?v=VzGAYNKDyIU.

"Bible Commentary." Bible Commentary | United Church of God. Accessed June 15, 2017. http://bible.ucg.org/.

"Bible Hub: Search, Read, Study the Bible in Many Languages." Bible Hub: Search, Read, Study the Bible in Many Languages. Accessed June 15, 2017. http://biblehub.com/.

Black, Duncan, Robert Groves, Helen Hucker, Cormac McKeown, Elaine Higgleton, and Lucy Cooper. Collins dictionary. Glasgow: HarperCollins Publishers, 2009.

CarrieunderwoodVEVO. "Carrie Underwood - Something in the Water." YouTube. November 06, 2014. Accessed June 15, 2017. http://www.youtube.com/watch?v=mH9kYn4L8TI.

CastingCrowns. "Casting Crowns - Courageous [Official Music Video - HD]." YouTube. June 21, 2011. Accessed June 15, 2017. http://www.youtube.com/watch?v=pkM-gDcmJeM

CastingCrownsVEVO. "Casting Crowns - Thrive (Official Lyric Video)." YouTube. December 18, 2013. Accessed June 15, 2017. http://www.youtube.com/watch?v=qQ71RWJhS_M.

ChrisTomlinVEVO. "Chris Tomlin - Whom Shall I Fear [God of Angel Armies] [Lyrics]." YouTube. October 29, 2012. Accessed June 15, 2017. http://www.youtube.com/watch?v=qOkImV2cJDg.

Desertbob61. "Casting Crowns - East to West." YouTube. September 05, 2007. Accessed June 15, 2017. http://www.youtube.com/watch?v=WyoVJfADlwo.

"Fairfax County Public Schools." Home | Fairfax County Public Schools. Accessed June 15, 2017. https://www.fcps.edu/.

Grimes, Nikki, Don Williams, Jim Story, and H. R. Russell. Walt Disneys Cinderella. New York: Random House, 2005.

Henry, Matthew. Matthew Henrys Concise Commentary on the whole Bible. Nashville: T. Nelson, 1997.

Hitchcock, Mark. The complete book of Bible prophecy. Wheaton, IL: Tyndale House Publishers, 1999.

Integritymusic. ""Made New" from Lincoln Brewster (OFFICIAL LYRIC VIDEO)." YouTube. July 21, 2014. Accessed June 15, 2017. http://www.youtube.com/watch?v=jd4qtmDGIWQ.

Jameseow. "In Christ Alone - Travis Cottrell." YouTube. August 10, 2007. Accessed June 15, 2017. http://www.youtube.com/watch?v=ZFzsU6u853I.

Jordanhieber1. "Newsboys - Overflow." YouTube. September 09, 2013. Accessed June 15, 2017. http://www.youtube.com/watch?v=kxN48r_nDB0.

"Kutless Lyrics - Better Is One Day." Accessed June 15, 2017. http://www.bing.com/cr?IG=E94189E0B4644F57A1D8C220B7AE05A2&CID=0F8907B20A-936C5A15710D100B956D20&rd=1&h=6T4XwA0FAKLST8dlYRmrvjPt-mGl0mRQkVIV5B6pcf3A&v=1&r=http%3a%2f%2fwww.azlyrics.com%2flyrics%2fkutless%2fbetterisoneday.html&p=DevEx,5533.1.

Lang, J. Stephen. Guideposts know the Bible in 30 days: discovering historical facts, biblical insights, and the inspiring power of Gods Word. New York: Guideposts, 2008.

Larfm1. "Casting Crowns--Wedding Day with lyrics." YouTube. October 23, 2011. Accessed June 15, 2017. http://www.youtube.com/watch?v=S_as9yxrf6E.

Lucado, Max, and Sergio Martinez. You are special. Oxford: Candle Books, 2015.

McClelland, James. Great hymns of faith. Belfast: Exeter, 1989.

McGee, J. Vernon. Thru the Bible commentary series. Nashville: T. Nelson, 1991.

MatthewWestVEVO. "Matthew West - Grace Wins." YouTube. December 03, 2015. Accessed June 15, 2017. http://www.youtube.com/watch?v=3a1WKcB7umU.

Mikeschairtv. ""Someone Worth Dying For" - MIKESCHAIR OFFICIAL (High Quality)." YouTube. April 29, 2011. Accessed June 15, 2017. http://www.youtube.com/watch?v=KSoAkJXjxiU.

Moore, Beth. Breaking free: day by day. Nashville, TN: B & H Publishing Group, 2007.

Moore, Beth. Children of the day: 1 & 2 Thessalonians. Nashville, TN: Lifeway Press, 2014.

Moore, Beth. Jesus: 90 days with the One and Only. Nashville, TN: B & H Publishing Group, 2007.

Morgan, Rachel. "A History of Wedding Veils - Styles and trends through the ages." Wedding Ideas. July 19, 2012. Accessed June 15, 2017. https://www.weddingideas-mag.com/history-of-wedding-veils-styles-and-trends/.

"Music, Songs & Lyrics." Lyrics containing the term: even so come feat chris tomlin by passion. Accessed June 15, 2017. http://www.lyrics.com/lyrics/even%20so%20come%20feat%20chris%20tomlin%20by%20passion.

Nataliegrantvideos. "Natalie Grant - Clean (Live)." YouTube. October 25, 2015. Accessed June 15, 2017. http://www.youtube.com/watch?v=5ol1V-sj1gc.

Oberacker, Betty. The preludes of the Well-tempered clavier, volume I, Johann Sebastian Bach: a commentary and analysis. Ann Arbor, MI: University Microfilms International, 1986.

OConnor, Jane, and Robin Preiss-Glasser. Fancy Nancy: Bonjour, butterfly. New York, NY: Harper, 2012. PhillipCraigDeanVEVO.

"Phillips, Craig & Dean - Jesus, Only Jesus (Official Lyric Video)." YouTube. August 25, 2014. Accessed June 15, 2017. http://www.youtube.com/watch?v=boGXE4k3qpI.

Pgrassojr. "Phillips Craig & Dean - Amazed (Worship with Lyrics)." YouTube. November 11, 2009. Accessed June 15, 2017. http://www.youtube.com/watch?v=D9S86nMqaLg.

Rhony72. "Carrie Underwood - How Great Thou Art." YouTube. April 06, 2008. Accessed June 15, 2017. http://www.youtube.com/watch?v=nhvaDJTUmrU.

Richardet, Susan Kay. Finding the road less traveled. Place of publication not identified: Lulu Com, 2014.

Rogers, Adrian, and Steve Rogers. What Every Christian Ought to Know. Nashville: B & H Publishing Group, 2014.

SanctusRealVEVO. "Sanctus Real - Head In The Fight (Audio)." YouTube. October 07, 2014. Accessed June 15, 2017. http://www.youtube.com/watch?v=mielZFiLt_4.

Schmobot. "Johann Pachelbel - Canon in D Major." YouTube. June 26, 2007. Accessed June 15, 2017. http://www.youtube.com/watch?v=8Af372EQLck.

SparrowRecords. "Matthew West - Unchangeable Lyrics." YouTube. October 01, 2012. Accessed June 15, 2017. http://www.youtube.com/watch?v=dm208V3g7UY.

TheAnimaSeries. "What Are You Afraid Of? - Jon Jorgenson." YouTube. December 13, 2013. Accessed June 15, 2017. http://www.youtube.com/watch?v=HZIr85Rxln0.

"The Christian Bible Reference Site - Home Page." Christian Bible Reference Site. Accessed June 15, 2017. http://christianbiblereference.org/.

The family man (Motion picture: 2000). Directed by Brett Ratner.

"Urban - Dictionary Definition." Vocabulary.com. Accessed June 15, 2017. https://www.vocabulary.com/dictionary/urban.

Verbrugge, Verlyn D., and Dirk R. Buursma. NIV topical study Bible: New International Version. Grand Rapids, MI, U.S.A.: Zondervan Bible Publishers, 1989.

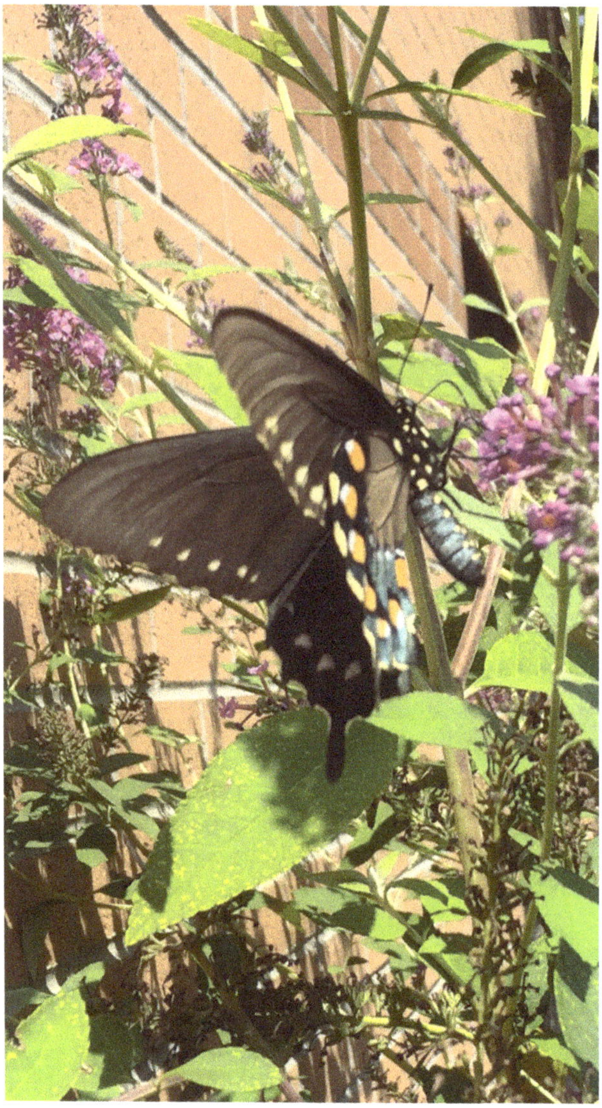

ABOUT THE AUTHOR

Gina New Shumpert is a writer, teacher, mother, and grandmother who spends her days looking for the hidden treasures God has placed along her path (Isa. 45:3). Gina and her husband, Jera, reside in Powder Springs, Georgia, where they raised their family who now have families of their own. They are devoted to their local congregation of Westside Christian Church in Hiram, Georgia.

Gina has spent over twenty-one years teaching elementary-aged students in Acworth, Georgia. Her life is filled with many adventures such as running 5Ks to marathons, kayaking, wave runner riding, and participating in YMCA classes—but, most importantly, snuggling with her grandbabies.

CPSIA information can be obtained
at www.ICGtesting.com
Printed in the USA
BVHW020555150319
542741BV00001B/1/P